I0008077

THE FAITH MEDIA REVOLUTION

Uniting Social, Streaming, Broadcast, and Cable for Maximum Outreach

Lee Allen Miller

Copyright © 2025 MSG Books | Lee Allen Miller

THE FAITH MEDIA REVOLUTION

Uniting Social, Streaming, Broadcast, and Cable for Maximum Outreach

All rights reserved.

Published by
MSG Books
1511 S Chestnut St
Lufkin, TX 75901

Kindle ISBN: 979-8-9921074-1-8
Paperback ISBN: 979-8-9921074-2-5

No part of this publication may be reproduced, stored in a retrieval system, or transmitted in any form or by any means, electronic, mechanical, photocopying, recording, scanning, or otherwise, except as permitted under Section 107 or 108 of the 1976 United States Copyright Act, without either the prior written permission of the publisher or author. Scripture quotations are taken from the Holy Bible, New International Version®, NIV®. Copyright © 1973, 1978, 1984, 2011 by Biblica, Inc.™ Used by permission of Zondervan. All rights reserved worldwide. Limit of Liability/Disclaimer of Warranty: While the publisher and author have used their best efforts in preparing this book, they make no representations or warranties with respect to the accuracy or completeness of the contents of this book. The advice and strategies contained herein may not be suitable for your situation. You should consult with a professional where appropriate. Neither the publisher nor the author shall be liable for any loss of profit or any other commercial damages, including but not limited to special, incidental, consequential, personal, or other damages.

For information about special discounts for bulk purchases or speaking engagements, please contact MSG Books at info@msgpr.com or 936-637-7593.

Printed in the United States of America
First Edition: 2025

Contents

Introduction: The Faith Media Revolution

The Digital Media Mandate

For centuries, the church has been a leader in communication, from handwritten scrolls to the printing press, from radio to television. Yet today, as digital media reshapes how people engage with information, many ministries and faith-based media leaders find themselves struggling to keep up. Traditional outreach methods are no longer enough. Social media, streaming, broadcast, and cable must work together to create a unified and impactful media presence. This isn't just a shift—it's a revolution.

The world is no longer passively consuming content; it is engaging, interacting, and expecting connection. Ministries that fail to adapt will find themselves increasingly disconnected from their audience. But those who embrace the digital transformation will see unprecedented growth in outreach, engagement, and impact.

Why Ministries Must Adapt or Fade

The modern faith audience is not waiting for a Sunday sermon. They are scrolling through social media, watching content on-demand, and engaging with multiple forms of media throughout the day. They seek authenticity, connection, and content that speaks to their lives in real time.

The statistics are clear:

- Over **4.9 billion people** worldwide use social media.
- **80% of internet users** watch video content weekly.
- **Live streaming has surged by 99%** in recent years.

- **Traditional TV and radio** still maintain influence but must evolve to remain relevant.

Faith-based organizations that cling to outdated media models will lose relevance. Those that embrace digital-first strategies will thrive. This book is your guide to leading that change.

Who This Book is For

This book is for faith-driven leaders ready to integrate **social media, streaming, broadcast, and cable** into a powerhouse media strategy. Whether you are a:

- **Church and Ministry Leader** seeking to expand your message beyond Sunday services.
- **Broadcaster or Media Executive** looking to blend digital-first strategies with traditional platforms.
- **Nonprofit Communicator or Marketer** wanting to grow your audience and donors.
- **Social Media Manager or Digital Content Creator** navigating the evolving media landscape.
- **Entrepreneur in Faith-Based Media** wanting to launch and scale influence.
- **Tech Leader or Innovator** interested in AI, Web3, and emerging media trends.

If you recognize the urgency of digital transformation and want to take action, this book is for you.

The Core Thesis of This Book

All people need Jesus, and in today's media-driven world, ministries must leverage **all available media channels**—social, streaming, broadcast, and cable—to effectively reach and engage audiences. Yet many struggle to integrate these platforms, over-relying on one while neglecting others.

This book presents a **practical, step-by-step guide** to blending digital and traditional media into a **seamless, high-impact outreach model**. By repurposing content and optimizing platform strengths, ministries can extend their reach, foster deeper engagement, and build a sustainable, powerhouse media presence that shares the Gospel worldwide.

What You'll Learn in This Book

Each chapter in this book will provide you with **actionable strategies** to maximize your outreach:

- **Developing a Unified Media Strategy**: How to balance social, streaming, broadcast, and cable for cohesive messaging.
- **The Art of Storytelling Across Media**: Creating compelling content that resonates across different platforms.
- **Social Media as the New Front Door of the Church**: Leveraging Facebook, YouTube, TikTok, and Instagram for outreach.
- **The Power of Live Streaming**: Reaching global audiences and fostering real-time engagement.
- **Reinventing Traditional Broadcast & Cable**: Adapting legacy media to the digital-first world.
- **Monetization & Sustainability**: Funding your media strategy through digital giving, subscriptions, crowdfunding, and sponsorships.
- **The Future of Faith-Based Media**: AI, Web3, and emerging technologies shaping ministry outreach.
- **Implementation Roadmap**: A checklist and case studies to help you execute your media vision.

Each chapter includes **proven strategies, industry insights, and practical takeaways** to help you transform your approach to faith-based media.

The Inspiration Behind This Book

The inspiration for this project was a workshop at the National Religious Broadcasters Convention in February 2025 in Dallas. As the moderator, I had the privilege of leading a panel discussion with three powerhouses in the Christian media world. Their expertise, insights, and visionary approaches to faith-based media integration laid the foundation for many of the strategies and principles outlined in this book. While this book was written before the workshop took place, I have drawn from the panelists' writings and industry expertise to craft a guide that will help ministries, broadcasters, and content creators navigate the evolving media landscape. See Reference page at end.

A Call to Action: Join the Faith Media Revolution

This is more than just a book—it's a movement.

Faith leaders today stand at a crossroads: cling to outdated media methods or step boldly into the future. The time to act is now. Ministries and leaders who hesitate will find themselves left behind. Those who embrace this revolution will see their impact multiply beyond what they ever imagined.

Every chapter in this book is designed to **equip you with the tools, strategies, and confidence** to unify social, streaming, broadcast, and cable into a **cohesive powerhouse media strategy**.

Are you ready to take the leap? Are you prepared to **lead the charge in faith-based media transformation**?

This book will show you how.

Welcome to **The Faith Media Revolution**.

1 The Digital Media Mandate

The Faith Media Landscape – Why Integration Matters

A Fractured Message in a Noisy World

In 2020, a well-known ministry launched a groundbreaking online sermon series, anticipating a surge in engagement. They invested in social media ads, uploaded videos to YouTube, aired programs on their local Christian television network, and even secured a weekly radio spot. Yet, after six months, engagement remained stagnant. Frustrated, their leadership team scrambled for answers. What went wrong?

The problem wasn't their message—it was their strategy. Each platform operated in isolation. Their YouTube audience had no connection to their TV broadcast. Social media posts promoted the sermons but lacked compelling storytelling. Radio listeners never knew about their digital resources. Instead of a **unified outreach**, they had **scattered efforts**, each failing to build momentum.

9

This scenario isn't unique. Countless faith-based organizations struggle with a **fragmented media approach**, limiting their impact in an era where attention is divided across platforms. The solution? **Integration.**

The Challenge of a Disconnected Media Presence

For decades, Christian outreach followed a clear structure: Sunday sermons, midweek Bible studies, and radio or television broadcasts for extended reach. The rise of digital media, however, disrupted this predictable rhythm. Now, audiences consume content on-demand—scrolling through Instagram, binge-watching faith-based content on streaming services, and interacting with real-time discussions on Twitter and YouTube.

This shift creates **two major challenges** for faith-based media leaders:

1. **Scattered Attention** – People no longer follow a single platform. They switch between social media, streaming, and traditional media, often within minutes.
2. **Platform-Specific Consumption** – What works on cable TV does not translate seamlessly to a YouTube series. A well-crafted Instagram post may be invisible on a broadcast network.

Without integration, faith-based media leaders risk losing their audience to disconnection, confusion, or irrelevance.

Integration: The Key to Sustainable Outreach

The most effective ministries today don't just exist across multiple platforms—they seamlessly connect them into a **single, cohesive experience.**

When faith leaders **integrate** social, streaming, broadcast, and cable, they create a **unified content ecosystem** where:

- A short Instagram video teases an upcoming message on a streaming platform.
- Livestreamed sermons feed into a podcast for on-the-go listening.
- Cable TV programs invite viewers to continue the conversation through an online community.

This strategy transforms outreach from **a series of isolated efforts into a synchronized journey that nurtures deeper engagement.**

Consider the case of **Pathway to Victory**, one of the most successful faith-based media brands. By embracing integration, they have maintained **36 consecutive months as the top-rated show on the Trinity Broadcasting Network (TBN).** They don't just broadcast—they create a continuous experience across multiple platforms, keeping audiences engaged **wherever they are.**

The Cost of Ignoring Media Integration

What happens when faith-based organizations fail to adapt?

- **Declining Engagement** – Ministries reliant only on traditional media see **dwindling viewership** as audiences shift to digital-first habits.
- **Wasted Resources** – Content repurposed poorly across platforms leads to **misaligned messaging** and lower ROI.
- **Missed Opportunities** – Younger audiences expect cross-platform engagement. Without it, faith-based organizations lose touch with future generations.

A prime example is a once-thriving faith-based TV network that resisted streaming and social media, believing its traditional audience would remain loyal. Within five years, viewership dropped **over 40%**, advertising revenue plummeted, and they scrambled to launch digital initiatives—too late to regain lost ground.

Building a Media Ecosystem: A Roadmap for Faith Leaders

How can ministries and media leaders successfully integrate their media presence?

1. Align Messaging Across All Platforms

Your message should be **consistent yet tailored** to each platform:

- A **Sunday sermon** becomes a **podcast episode** for deeper reflection.
- A **30-minute broadcast** is broken into **bite-sized YouTube clips**.
- A **social media post** drives traffic to a **full-length teaching on a streaming platform**.

2. Leverage Platform Strengths Instead of Copy-Pasting Content

Each media channel has unique strengths. Instead of repurposing the same content verbatim, adapt it for the audience's behavior:

- **Social Media:** Short, engaging clips with direct interaction.
- **Streaming:** On-demand, binge-worthy deep dives.
- **Broadcast TV:** Trust-building and credibility through long-form storytelling.

- **Cable Networks:** High-quality production targeting specific demographics.

3. Build a Cross-Platform Engagement Funnel

Your audience should move **seamlessly between platforms.** For example:

- A YouTube sermon leads viewers to **join a live discussion** on Facebook.
- A TV special promotes a **weekly podcast for more in-depth insights**.
- A live-streamed event integrates **real-time social media interactions**.

4. Adopt Data-Driven Strategies

Track engagement trends and audience behavior across platforms:

- **Which platforms drive the most engagement?**
- **What content formats are most effective?**
- **How do viewers transition between media channels?**

By **analyzing audience behavior**, ministries can optimize efforts **for maximum impact**.

The Future of Faith-Based Media

Faith-based media is at a crossroads. Those who continue to **operate in silos** will struggle. Those who **integrate with**

purpose will thrive. **The world is listening—but only to those who speak in a way they can hear.**

As you move forward in this book, you'll discover **how faith audiences are shifting** (*Chapter 1.2: The Shifting Media Habits of Faith Audiences*) and how to structure content for **maximum engagement across platforms.**

The question is not **whether** integration is necessary—it's whether faith-based leaders are ready to embrace the challenge.

Are you?

The Digital Transformation of Faith-Based Media

The Shift from Traditional to Digital: A Necessary Evolution

Faith-based media has long been a cornerstone of outreach, using print, radio, and television to spread the message of hope, inspiration, and transformation. However, in today's rapidly evolving digital landscape, traditional methods alone are no longer sufficient. Ministries and faith-based organizations must embrace digital transformation—not as an optional addition but as an essential strategy for survival and growth.

Digital transformation is more than just adopting new technology—it's a fundamental shift in how ministries communicate, engage, and build relationships with their audiences. The rise of social media, streaming platforms, and on-demand digital content has changed the way people consume information and interact with faith-based messages. To remain relevant and effective, organizations must integrate digital tools into their outreach strategies while maintaining the authenticity and personal connection that defines faith-based communication.

Understanding the Challenges of Integration

While the need for digital transformation is clear, many faith-based organizations struggle to unify their efforts across social media, streaming, broadcast, and cable. Common challenges include:

- **Over-reliance on Traditional Media**: Many churches and ministries still focus primarily on television or radio, missing the opportunity to engage audiences where they are—online.
- **Lack of a Unified Strategy**: Content is often created for one platform without consideration for how it can be repurposed and distributed across multiple channels.
- **Fear of Technology**: Some leaders hesitate to adopt new digital tools due to unfamiliarity or misconceptions about their effectiveness.
- **Engagement vs. Broadcasting Mindset**: Traditional media has been about pushing messages out, while digital media thrives on interaction and engagement. Many ministries still struggle to shift from one-way communication to meaningful dialogue.

By addressing these challenges, faith-based organizations can move beyond isolated efforts and build a cohesive, powerful outreach strategy.

The Power of an Integrated Approach

A true digital transformation involves **unifying** social, streaming, broadcast, and cable into a **single, seamless strategy**. Instead of treating each platform as a separate entity, ministries should view them as complementary tools that work together to enhance reach, deepen engagement, and maximize impact.

Social Media: The Front Door to Faith-Based Engagement

Social media is where first impressions are made. For many people, their first interaction with a ministry will happen on Facebook, Instagram, YouTube, or TikTok—not in a church building. This is why **social media should be treated as the "front door" of ministry outreach**.

- **Consistent Posting and Engagement**: Churches and ministries must maintain an active presence by posting regularly and responding to comments and messages.
- **Storytelling That Resonates**: Authentic, relatable content—testimonies, behind-the-scenes looks, and interactive posts—connect with audiences better than formal announcements.
- **Leveraging Paid Reach**: Platforms like Facebook and Instagram offer affordable advertising options that allow ministries to extend their reach to targeted audiences.

Streaming: Creating a Digital Sanctuary

Streaming is no longer just an add-on to in-person services; it has become a primary way people experience faith-based content. Whether through YouTube, Facebook Live, or dedicated church streaming platforms, streaming allows ministries to reach a **global audience** in real time.

- **Live Services & Interactive Features**: Encouraging viewers to comment, share prayer requests, and engage in discussion fosters a sense of community.
- **On-Demand Content for Accessibility**: Making past sermons, Bible studies, and faith-based teachings available on-demand allows audiences to consume content at their convenience.

- **Expanding Beyond Sunday Services**: Midweek devotionals, Q&A sessions, and live worship experiences keep engagement high throughout the week.

Broadcast & Cable: Reaching Established Audiences

Despite the rapid shift to digital, television remains a powerful medium for faith-based outreach. Many older audiences and rural communities still rely on **traditional broadcasting** to access spiritual content.

- **Repurposing Sermons and Teachings**: Churches can air condensed versions of sermons and devotionals on local TV networks.
- **Hybrid Approaches**: Ministries can integrate calls to action that drive viewers to online platforms for deeper engagement.
- **Expanding to Faith-Based Networks**: Platforms like TBN and Daystar provide additional opportunities for ministries to share their message.

Key Strategies for Unifying Media Outreach

To create a truly unified outreach strategy, ministries and faith-based media organizations must take a strategic, intentional approach. Here are key principles to follow:

1. Develop a Cohesive Content Strategy

Content should be created with **multi-platform distribution in mind**. Instead of treating each medium separately, ministries should develop a **content funnel** that allows a single piece of content to be adapted for multiple channels.

For example:

- A sermon can be live-streamed on Sunday → Edited into a 30-minute TV broadcast → Broken into short clips for social media → Transcribed into a blog post → Discussed in a live Q&A session.

By planning content with repurposing in mind, ministries can **maximize their resources and reach**.

2. Prioritize Authentic Storytelling

Phil Cooke, a leader in faith-based media, emphasizes that ministries must **break free from outdated, rigid content formats** and embrace storytelling that connects with contemporary audiences. People are drawn to **real, raw, and relatable content** rather than polished, overly formal presentations.

Ministries should:

- **Share testimonies**: Personal stories of faith journeys resonate deeply.
- **Embrace behind-the-scenes content**: Show the human side of ministry.
- **Encourage user-generated content**: Invite the community to share their experiences.

3. Engage, Don't Just Broadcast

Social media and streaming require a shift from **one-way broadcasting to two-way engagement**. Ministries must build a culture of **conversation** by:

- Responding to comments and messages in real time.
- Encouraging discussion through polls, questions, and interactive content.
- Offering live prayer and engagement opportunities.

4. Use Data to Optimize Outreach

Successful digital outreach isn't just about posting content—it's about **measuring impact and making data-driven decisions**.

Key metrics to track:

- **Engagement Rates**: Comments, shares, and likes indicate how well content resonates.
- **Watch Time**: Understanding how long people watch a video can reveal what's effective.
- **Conversion Rates**: Tracking how many people take action (e.g., signing up for a newsletter or attending an event).

Ministries that use **analytics tools** can adjust their strategies to maximize impact.

5. Leverage Emerging Technology

Nils Smith, a leading voice in digital ministry, emphasizes that ministries must **lean into technology** rather than fear it. Innovations such as **AI, Web3, and blockchain** are shaping the future of digital outreach.

- **AI for Personalized Engagement**: Chatbots and AI-driven tools can help respond to audience questions and prayer requests efficiently.
- **Web3 and Digital Giving**: Cryptocurrencies and blockchain-based donation platforms are emerging as new methods for funding ministry initiatives.
- **Virtual and Augmented Reality**: These technologies create immersive worship and discipleship experiences.

By **embracing technology**, ministries can position themselves at the forefront of digital engagement.

Embracing the Future of Faith-Based Media

The journey from traditional media to a fully integrated digital outreach strategy requires **intentionality, adaptability, and boldness**. Faith-based organizations that successfully unify social media, streaming, broadcast, and cable will **not only expand their reach but also build deeper, more meaningful relationships with their audiences**.

As we move forward in this transformation, ministries must remember that digital tools are **not just about technology—they're about people**. The heart of faith-based outreach remains the same: **connecting people with the message of hope and transformation**. The difference today is that **we now have more ways than ever to reach them**.

This digital revolution is not a threat—it is an opportunity. Ministries and media leaders who embrace it will **not only survive but thrive** in the new era of faith-based communication.

2 Foundations of a Unified Media Strategy

The Power of Integration – How a Unified Approach Transforms Outreach

The Challenge: Fragmented Outreach Efforts

In today's fast-paced media landscape, faith-based organizations face an overwhelming number of platforms and technologies. Some churches and ministries pour all their efforts into social media but fail to recognize the enduring power of television and radio. Others invest heavily in traditional broadcasting while neglecting the engagement opportunities available through livestreaming and on-demand content. The result? A fragmented outreach strategy that limits potential impact.

The challenge is clear: Many faith-based organizations struggle to integrate these platforms cohesively, often over-relying on one while neglecting others. This siloed approach creates inconsistencies in messaging, disconnects audiences, and diminishes effectiveness.

The solution? A unified approach—one that blends social media, streaming, broadcast, and cable into a seamless outreach model. When properly integrated, these channels work together to reinforce messaging, expand reach, and foster deeper engagement with audiences.

Why Integration Matters

A ministry's mission is to connect people with the Gospel. In an era where attention is divided among multiple platforms, a single-medium approach is no longer sufficient. Integration matters because:

1. **Audiences are everywhere** – Some members of your community prefer watching traditional TV, while others consume content via YouTube, podcasts, or Facebook Live. A single-channel approach excludes potential viewers.
2. **Repetition builds retention** – Marketing studies show that people need multiple touchpoints before engaging with content. By uniting various platforms, ministries ensure their message is reinforced across multiple mediums.
3. **Each platform serves a unique purpose** – Social media excels at engagement, streaming at accessibility, broadcast at credibility, and cable at longevity. A strategic combination of these platforms creates a holistic outreach effort.
4. **A unified message increases impact** – Fragmented efforts create inconsistencies. An integrated strategy aligns messaging across all media, ensuring a coherent and powerful voice.

The Consequences of a Disconnected Strategy

To illustrate the power of integration, consider two ministries:

Ministry A: The Fragmented Approach

Ministry A operates a local Christian TV broadcast, but its website is outdated, and its social media is inactive. It only posts sermon clips sporadically on YouTube and never engages with online audiences. The result? Limited viewership, declining engagement, and a struggle to attract younger audiences.

Ministry B: The Unified Approach

Ministry B, on the other hand, understands the importance of integration. It live-streams services weekly, repurposes sermon highlights for social media, interacts with viewers in real-time, and ensures that its traditional broadcast efforts reinforce its digital initiatives. As a result, it sees growth in engagement, a broader audience, and increased donor support.

The difference? One ministry operates in silos, while the other embraces a cohesive media strategy that maximizes its outreach potential.

Expert Insights on Integration

Phil Cooke: The Power of Storytelling Across Platforms

Phil Cooke, a renowned media consultant, emphasizes the need for compelling storytelling that resonates across all platforms. He warns against outdated language and approaches, urging ministries to communicate in ways that connect with modern audiences. According to Cooke, many faith-based organizations struggle because they fail to adapt their message for digital-first audiences.

"In a media-driven culture, we need to do a better job of telling our story."

Ministries that master storytelling across broadcast, social, and streaming channels create a deeper emotional connection with their audience, ensuring their message is both engaging and memorable.

Michael Clarke: Bridging Traditional and Digital Broadcasting

Michael Clarke, Executive Director of Pathway to Victory, has led a faith-based media organization to achieve record viewership. He underscores the importance of blending traditional broadcast with digital tools, ensuring that legacy media and emerging platforms complement rather than compete with one another.

Pathway to Victory's success lies in its ability to maintain a strong presence on television while embracing streaming and social media. Clarke's strategy illustrates how ministries can amplify their impact by integrating various media channels.

Nils Smith: The Role of AI and Web3 in Integration

Nils Smith, Chief Strategist of Social Media and Innovation at Dunham + Company, champions the role of emerging technologies in outreach. He advocates for:

- Leveraging AI for content personalization.
- Using Web3 and blockchain for innovative fundraising.
- Creating interactive digital experiences to increase engagement.

By integrating AI-driven strategies with traditional media, ministries can enhance audience interactions and streamline content distribution across multiple platforms.

Practical Steps to Achieve Integration

1. **Audit Your Current Media Presence**
   - Identify strengths and gaps in your media strategy.
   - Determine which platforms need more investment.
2. **Develop a Cohesive Content Plan**
   - Align messaging across social media, streaming, broadcast, and cable.
   - Create a content calendar to ensure consistent posting.
3. **Repurpose Content for Multiple Platforms**
   - Turn sermons into blog posts, podcasts, and social media clips.
   - Adapt long-form video content for short-form engagement on platforms like Instagram and TikTok.
4. **Invest in Engagement, Not Just Broadcasting**
   - Respond to comments, interact with followers, and create community-driven content.
   - Use live Q&A sessions, polls, and interactive features to foster deeper connections.
5. **Embrace Technology for Better Outreach**
   - Utilize AI for content recommendations and chatbots for real-time engagement.
   - Experiment with digital giving platforms and NFTs for fundraising.

The Transformational Shift

By moving from a fragmented to a unified media approach, ministries will experience:

- **Stronger audience engagement.**
- **Increased reach across generations and demographics.**

- **More sustainable media strategies that maximize content investment.**
- **A cohesive and impactful digital ministry.**

The goal is not to abandon traditional methods but to enhance and unite them with modern tools. Ministries that embrace integration will not only survive in the evolving media landscape but will thrive, reaching audiences with greater depth and effectiveness.

A Call to Action

Faith-based media leaders are at a crossroads: They can either remain siloed in outdated methods or embrace the full potential of a unified media strategy. The time to act is now. By integrating social media, streaming, broadcast, and cable into a single, cohesive approach, ministries can create a powerhouse outreach that transforms lives.

This is the foundation for the future of faith-based media—a future where technology, storytelling, and engagement work together to share the Gospel more effectively than ever before.

Implementing a Unified Media Strategy for Maximum Outreach

The Next Step: Moving from Concept to Execution

In the previous chapter, we explored **why uniting social, streaming, broadcast, and cable is essential for effective outreach**. Now, we take the next step—**how to actually implement a unified media strategy that reaches, engages, and transforms audiences**.

Too many faith-based organizations struggle to integrate their media efforts cohesively. Some **over-rely on traditional**

television broadcasts, others focus heavily on **social media while neglecting cable or streaming platforms**. The key is to stop viewing each channel as separate and instead, **blend them into a seamless, high-impact communication strategy**.

This chapter will provide **clear, step-by-step methods to execute a unified approach**—one that maintains the heart of your mission while leveraging modern media tools.

The Core of Integration: A Single Message Across Multiple Platforms

A strong, unified media strategy is not about repeating the same content word-for-word on every platform. It's about **communicating the same message in ways that fit each medium's unique audience and strengths**.

Imagine a pastor delivering a **sermon on faith**. Instead of broadcasting the same hour-long sermon across all platforms, here's how that message can be **repurposed strategically**:

- **Social Media** (Instagram, TikTok, Facebook): Short-form video clips (30–60 seconds) that highlight key points from the sermon.
- **Streaming Platforms (YouTube, Roku, Apple TV, etc.)**: Full-length, high-quality sermon video.
- **Cable and Broadcast TV**: A **30-minute edited version**, focusing on the most engaging and transformative parts.
- **Podcast or Radio Broadcast**: An **audio-only version**, allowing deeper conversation around the sermon topic.
- **Email and Blogs**: A **written breakdown**, including Scripture references and practical takeaways.

Key Takeaway: You don't have to create different messages for every platform—you just need to tailor the format and length to match each audience's behavior.

Building a Cross-Platform Content Strategy

A well-integrated media strategy doesn't happen by accident. It requires **intentional planning, structure, and execution**. Here's how to start:

1. Clarify Your Message

- What is the **core message** you want to share? (Example: "Faith in Uncertain Times")
- What is the **primary action** you want people to take? (Pray, subscribe, donate, attend an event?)
- How does this message fit into your broader **ministry goals**?

2. Define Your Audience on Each Platform

Different platforms reach different demographics. Understanding these differences **helps shape how you present your message**:

- **Social Media (YouTube, Facebook, Instagram, TikTok)** -Younger audience, fast engagement, short-form content.
- **Streaming Services (YouTube Live, Roku, Apple TV)** - Digital-savvy viewers, long-form content, interactive engagement.
- **Broadcast & Cable TV** - Older, traditional audience, storytelling-driven content.
- **Podcast & Radio** - Commuters, deep thinkers, long-form audio content.

3. Develop a Content Calendar

Once you've **defined your message** and **understood your audience**, it's time to **schedule content across all platforms in a synchronized way**:

- **Monday:** Release a **teaser video** on social media promoting the upcoming sermon.
- **Tuesday:** Publish a **blog post** with Scripture references and an introduction to the topic.
- **Wednesday:** Post a **behind-the-scenes or Q&A video** about the sermon.
- **Thursday:** Stream a **midweek devotional or testimonial** that supports the sermon message.
- **Friday:** Post a **short reflection video** on TikTok or Instagram Stories.
- **Sunday:** Broadcast the **full-length sermon on TV, streaming, and podcast**.
- **Monday:** Repurpose clips from Sunday's message into **short-form content** for next week.

4. Engage Your Audience Across Platforms

Integration is **not just about broadcasting**—it's about **creating engagement loops**:

- Include **QR codes in TV broadcasts** that drive people to your social media or website.
- Use **YouTube end screens** to direct viewers to watch your live stream.
- Encourage social media users to **subscribe to your email list** for deeper content.
- Use **text message alerts** to remind people of upcoming broadcasts.

The goal is to **lead people from one platform to another**, keeping them engaged in your ministry throughout the week.

The "Content Flywheel" – How One Piece of Content Fuels Everything Else

Instead of creating **separate content** for every platform, **repurpose and optimize** one core message across multiple mediums. This creates a **content flywheel**—a system where each piece of content fuels the next.

1. **Record your sermon or keynote message** → Upload the full version to streaming & broadcast.
2. **Break the full version into shorter clips** → Share on social media.
3. **Extract the audio** → Publish as a podcast episode.
4. **Convert key points into a blog post** → Add SEO keywords for better reach.
5. **Use sermon notes to create an email newsletter** → Provide additional resources.
6. **Gather audience feedback** → Use insights to improve next week's content.

This method allows you to **reach different audiences with the same message**, maximizing efficiency and engagement.

Overcoming the Challenges of Media Integration

Many faith-based organizations resist integrating their media strategy because of **common barriers**. Here's how to overcome them:

- **"We don't have the budget."** → Start with what you have. **Smartphones, free social platforms, and simple editing software** can help you repurpose content effectively.

- **"We don't have a media team."** → Train volunteers, leverage church members with digital skills, and **use automation tools** like Hootsuite or Buffer.
- **"Our audience isn't online."** → While **traditional broadcast remains vital**, even **older demographics** are increasingly using YouTube, Facebook, and smart TVs for faith content.
- **"We don't know where to start."** → Start small. Pick **two core platforms** and expand as you grow.

Moving Forward: Your Next Steps

By now, you understand the **why and how of integrating social, streaming, broadcast, and cable** into a powerhouse outreach strategy. The key is **intentional execution**—taking one step at a time and building momentum.

Actionable Steps This Week:

1. Identify **one core message** for your next campaign or sermon.
2. Create **a simple content calendar** for repurposing that message.
3. Choose **two primary platforms** to start integrating (Example: YouTube + Social Media).
4. Test **engagement loops** (ex: TV broadcast linking to social media, or YouTube video directing to email signup).
5. Gather feedback, refine, and **expand your integration efforts**.

A **truly unified media strategy doesn't happen overnight**, but with **intentionality and faith**, your message will reach more lives than ever before. The next chapter will dive deeper into **advanced engagement strategies that take your outreach to the next level—turning viewers into committed community members.**

The Art of Storytelling Across Media

Why Storytelling is Essential in Faith-Based Media

Storytelling is the foundation of faith-based communication. Jesus himself used parables to communicate complex spiritual truths in ways that resonated with his audience. Today, ministries and faith-based media organizations must harness the same power of storytelling to connect with their audiences across social media, streaming, broadcast, and cable. A well-crafted story can transcend platforms, making faith relevant and personal in the digital age.

Audiences today are overwhelmed with content, and factual information alone is not enough to hold their attention. Stories engage emotions, making them more memorable and impactful. Whether through a 30-second TikTok clip, a 30-minute streaming documentary, or a prime-time broadcast segment, storytelling allows faith-based media to break through the noise and forge deeper connections.

Platform-Specific Storytelling Approaches

Each media platform requires a different approach to storytelling, and understanding these nuances is key to maximizing impact.

1. Social Media: Short-Form and Attention-Grabbing

- **What Works:** Bite-sized, emotionally compelling stories that engage users quickly.
- **Best Practices:**
  - Use Instagram Reels, TikTok, and Facebook Stories for micro-testimonies.
  - Employ engaging captions and subtitles to make content accessible.

o Create challenge-based storytelling (e.g., "Tell us how faith has impacted your life").

2. Streaming: Long-Form and Immersive

- **What Works:** In-depth storytelling that allows audiences to fully engage.
- **Best Practices:**
  - o Develop mini-documentaries showcasing personal faith journeys.
  - o Livestream events with a strong narrative arc.
  - o Integrate cinematic techniques for visual impact.

3. Broadcast & Cable: High-Production and Wide Reach

- **What Works:** Structured, polished storytelling that appeals to mass audiences.
- **Best Practices:**
  - o Utilize professional scripting and editing.
  - o Develop sermon series or faith-based talk shows.
  - o Partner with networks to syndicate compelling content.

4. Cross-Platform Storytelling: Adapting Narratives Across Media

- **Repurposing Strategies:**
  - o Transform a sermon into a social media clip, a podcast episode, and a streaming special.
  - o Use behind-the-scenes clips to engage audiences before a major broadcast.
  - o Maintain consistency in messaging while tailoring content to each medium.

Crafting a Compelling Narrative

Great stories follow a structure that naturally draws audiences in and keeps them engaged. Ministries can use this structure to create content that captivates and inspires action.

The Storytelling Formula:

1. **Problem:** Identify a relatable challenge or struggle.
2. **Struggle:** Show the journey through difficulty.
3. **Transformation:** Illustrate how faith played a role in overcoming adversity.
4. **Call to Action:** Invite audiences to engage, share, or take a next step in their faith journey.

By following this structure, ministries can ensure their messages resonate deeply across all platforms.

Practical Storytelling Techniques

Writing for Impact:

- Use conversational language that feels personal.
- Keep messages concise yet powerful.
- Ask thought-provoking questions to draw engagement.

Visual Storytelling:

- Use high-quality images and videos to enhance narratives.
- Incorporate testimonials and personal faith stories.
- Ensure content is visually optimized for mobile devices.

Emerging Tech in Storytelling:

- AI-driven editing tools can enhance production quality.
- Virtual reality (VR) and augmented reality (AR) can create immersive faith experiences.

- AI-generated subtitles and translations can broaden accessibility.

From Storytelling to Engagement

A compelling story is only effective if it leads to engagement. Ministries must go beyond passive content consumption and encourage active participation.

How to Drive Engagement Through Storytelling:

- **Encourage User-Generated Content:** Ask followers to share their faith stories.
- **Use Interactive Elements:** Polls, Q&As, and live discussions build community.
- **Make a Clear Call to Action:** Direct viewers to comment, share, or sign up for deeper engagement.

Storytelling as a Bridge to Connection

Mastering storytelling across social media, streaming, broadcast, and cable is essential for modern faith-based media. By crafting narratives that are authentic, platform-specific, and emotionally compelling, ministries can extend their reach and deepen their impact. As we transition into the next chapter on leveraging social media for outreach and engagement, we'll explore how to amplify these storytelling strategies to foster lasting community connections.

Lee Allen Miller

3 Social Media: The New Front Door of the Church

Leveraging Social Media for Outreach & Engagement

Social Media as the Digital Pulpit

The rise of social media has transformed how ministries and faith-based organizations connect with their communities. No longer confined to physical spaces, churches, ministries, and faith-driven content creators can now reach audiences across the globe. But this new reality also brings challenges—how do you capture attention in an overcrowded digital space? How do you foster real engagement instead of passive consumption?

This chapter explores the principles of leveraging social media for outreach and engagement, offering practical strategies for faith leaders to maximize their impact.

Understanding Social Media as a Ministry Tool

For many churches, social media is an afterthought—an additional platform to share announcements or stream Sunday services. But this limited approach misses the real opportunity.

Social media is more than just a tool for promotion; it is a **dynamic space for discipleship, community-building, and storytelling**.

Key Insight: Social Media is a Two-Way Conversation

Unlike television, radio, or even traditional websites, social media thrives on interaction. Ministries that use it effectively engage in two-way conversations rather than simply broadcasting content. This means responding to comments, asking questions, and fostering discussions.

Quick Win: Start by replying to every comment on your ministry's posts for one month. Notice how engagement and relationships grow.

Choosing the Right Social Media Platforms

Each social platform has unique strengths. Ministries must choose the platforms that align best with their audience and goals.

Facebook – The Digital Community Hub

- Best for community building, live services, and group discussions.
- Facebook Groups offer a space for ongoing discipleship and prayer requests.

Instagram – Storytelling & Visual Engagement

- Great for short devotional messages, scripture-based graphics, and testimonials.
- Stories & Reels provide high visibility for quick, impactful content.

YouTube – The Sermon Library & Teaching Platform

- A long-form content powerhouse, perfect for sermon archives and teaching series.
- Live streaming worship services and Q&A sessions can create deeper engagement.

TikTok – Reaching Younger Audiences

- Ideal for short, powerful faith-based messages (testimonies, inspirational clips).
- Offers an opportunity for viral outreach through trends and hashtags.

X (Twitter) – Thought Leadership & Quick Encouragement

- Effective for sharing daily scriptures, quick insights, and engaging with trending faith topics.
- Great for live interactions during events.

Pro Tip: Don't try to be everywhere at once. Focus on mastering one or two platforms before expanding.

The Pillars of Effective Social Media Outreach

For ministries to maximize their social media impact, they must balance three key pillars:

1. Consistency – Showing Up Regularly

- Posting sporadically leads to disengagement. Ministries must commit to a consistent posting schedule.

- **Action Step:** Create a 30-day content calendar with a mix of scripture posts, short videos, and engagement-driven questions.

2. Authenticity – Being Real, Not Just Polished

- People connect with authenticity, not perfection. Sharing behind-the-scenes moments, testimonies, and even struggles can build trust.
- **Example:** A pastor sharing a short video on a personal faith struggle will likely resonate more than a perfectly scripted sermon clip.

3. Engagement – Encouraging Community Participation

- Ministries should move beyond just posting content and focus on **responding, interacting, and involving** their audience.
- **Strategy:** Ask engaging questions. Instead of just posting a verse, ask: *"How does this verse apply to your life today?"*

Creating Content That Inspires Action

Effective social media content moves people from passive scrolling to active participation. Ministries should aim to create content that educates, inspires, and calls people to deeper engagement.

Types of Content for Maximum Engagement

Content Type	Best Platforms	Purpose
Short Devotionals	Instagram, TikTok, Facebook	Inspire daily reflection
Live Prayer Sessions	Facebook, YouTube, Instagram	Create real-time community
Testimonies	Instagram, TikTok, YouTube	Encourage faith-sharing
Interactive Polls	Instagram Stories, X (Twitter)	Drive engagement
Behind-the-Scenes	Instagram, Facebook Stories	Humanize leadership

Case Study: A small church in Texas saw a **300% increase in engagement** after launching weekly Instagram Stories featuring short, real-life testimonies.

Overcoming Common Social Media Challenges

"We Don't Have the Time or Resources"

- **Solution:** Batch-create content. Spend one afternoon recording 4-5 short devotional videos that can be posted throughout the month.

"We Don't Get Much Engagement"

- **Solution:** Focus on interactive content. End every post with a question or call to action.

"We're Not Sure What to Post"

- **Solution:** Follow the **Content Rule of Thirds**:

1. **Inspirational Content (Bible verses, testimonies) – 33%**
2. **Educational Content (sermon clips, teachings) – 33%**
3. **Engagement-Driven Content (polls, Q&As, live discussions) – 33%**

Measuring Success: Beyond Likes & Follows

While follower count and likes can be encouraging, they are **not** the best indicators of success. Ministries should focus on **meaningful engagement metrics**:

Key Performance Indicators (KPIs) for Social Media Ministry

KPI	Why It Matters
Comments & Shares	Measures community engagement
Message Responses	Tracks direct impact on individuals
Live Stream Attendance	Shows depth of connection
Conversion Rate	How many people take the next step (attend a service, join a group)

Pro Tip: Don't just count audience size. Count the number of **real connections** you make.

Social Media as a Mission Field

Social media is not just an **add-on** to ministry; it is a **mission field** that requires intentionality, strategy, and faithfulness. Ministries that commit to leveraging social media effectively can build **thriving digital communities**, reach people who may never step into a church, and **turn passive viewers into active disciples**.

Reflection Questions:

1. What platform aligns best with my ministry's outreach goals?
2. How can I shift from "broadcasting" content to fostering two-way conversations?
3. What is one step I can take today to improve social media engagement?

Organic vs. Paid Growth Strategies

The Two Paths to Social Media Growth

Social media is the modern-day front door of the church, providing ministries with unparalleled opportunities for outreach and engagement. However, growing a ministry's digital presence requires more than just posting content—it requires a strategic approach. There are two main avenues for growth: **organic and paid strategies**. Understanding the strengths and weaknesses of each is essential for ministries seeking to maximize their reach and impact.

Organic growth refers to building an audience naturally through engagement, content sharing, and community interaction without spending money on ads. It's **authentic, sustainable, and deeply relational**, but it takes time and consistency. **Paid growth**, on the other hand, involves using advertising dollars to **boost visibility, target specific audiences, and accelerate engagement**. While effective, it requires careful budgeting and campaign management.

The key is **not choosing one over the other, but learning how to leverage both**. By blending organic engagement with targeted paid campaigns, ministries can **create a powerful social media presence that reaches the right people, at the right time, with the right message**.

Mastering Organic Growth: Engagement Over Algorithms

Organic growth is the foundation of **authentic ministry impact on social media**. It's about building a community, fostering relationships, and creating content that people want to share. Unlike paid ads, which provide immediate visibility, organic growth requires **consistent effort, creative content, and audience engagement**.

1. Create Value-Driven Content

Content is king in the digital age, but **engagement is the kingdom**. Ministries must focus on producing high-value content that resonates with their audience. This includes:

- **Sermon clips and Bible insights** – Bite-sized, inspirational content that encourages daily faith-based reflection.
- **Testimonies and real-life impact stories** – Personal narratives that connect emotionally and inspire sharing.
- **Behind-the-scenes content** – Authentic glimpses into the ministry, team, and daily work to foster connection.
- **Interactive posts** – Polls, Q&A sessions, and live discussions that invite participation.

2. Build a Two-Way Conversation

Social media should not be a **megaphone**, but a **dialogue**. Ministries must be intentional about engaging their followers by:

- **Responding to comments and messages** promptly.
- **Encouraging user-generated content**, such as members sharing their own testimonies.
- **Going live** for interactive Q&A sessions, prayer meetings, or devotionals.
- **Using calls-to-action** that invite discussion (e.g., "What's one way God has worked in your life this week?").

3. Leverage SEO and Social Media Optimization

- **Optimize your profile** with clear descriptions, keywords, and links to your website.
- Use **hashtags strategically** to increase discoverability.
- **Post at peak engagement times** to maximize reach (based on audience insights and analytics).

4. Stay Consistent and Authentic

- Develop a **content calendar** to maintain a steady posting schedule.
- Stick to a **consistent visual and messaging style** that aligns with your ministry's voice.
- **Prioritize authenticity over perfection**—genuine connection matters more than polished production.

Paid Growth: Investing in Kingdom Impact

While organic reach is powerful, social media algorithms often limit exposure. Paid strategies allow ministries to **break through algorithmic barriers, reach targeted demographics, and accelerate growth**.

1. Types of Social Media Ads

- **Boosted posts** – Amplify organic content to reach a larger audience.

- **Traffic ads** – Drive visitors to ministry websites, events, or donation pages.
- **Lead generation ads** – Collect contact information for newsletters and discipleship programs.
- **Video engagement ads** – Promote sermons, live streams, and video content to a wider audience.

2. Targeting Strategies for Faith-Based Audiences

Platforms like Facebook, Instagram, and YouTube allow ministries to **target their ideal audience** based on:

- **Demographics** (age, gender, location, language preferences).
- **Interests** (Christianity, faith-based books, worship music, specific church affiliations).
- **Behavioral data** (previous engagement with faith-based content, recent event attendance).
- **Lookalike audiences** – Reach new people similar to existing followers.

3. Budgeting for Social Media Ads

- **Start small, then scale** – Test different ad formats with a modest budget before investing heavily.
- **Monitor and optimize** – Track engagement, conversions, and audience response to refine ad performance.
- **Combine paid with organic** – Promote high-performing organic content with ad dollars to amplify impact.

4. Measuring ROI on Paid Campaigns

- **Engagement metrics** – Likes, shares, comments, and video views.
- **Conversion rates** – Click-through rates (CTR), event sign-ups, and donations.

- **Follower growth** – Increase in page likes and social media subscribers.
- **Cost per result** – Determine the efficiency of ad spending in reaching goals.

The Hybrid Approach: Maximizing Impact with Both Strategies

The most successful ministries don't rely solely on **organic or paid growth—they integrate both**. Here's how:

1. Repurpose High-Performing Organic Content

- Take top-performing organic posts and **turn them into paid ads** to reach a larger audience.
- Use **testimonials and sermon snippets** as ad creatives to drive engagement.
- Repackage **long-form videos into short, engaging clips** for both organic sharing and paid promotion.

2. Utilize AI for Enhanced Targeting *(a bridge to the next chapter on AI and Web3)*

- AI tools help **analyze engagement trends and optimize paid campaigns**.
- Algorithm-driven ad targeting ensures **cost-efficient spending**.
- Ministries can use **AI chatbots** to automate responses and enhance engagement.

3. Learn from Case Studies of Successful Ministries

- **Church A** used a combination of **Facebook Live and boosted event ads** to double attendance for online worship.

- **Ministry B** leveraged **organic discipleship content with retargeting ads** to increase donations by 40%.
- **Christian influencer C** optimized **YouTube SEO and sponsored ads** to grow a faith-based channel by 100K+ subscribers.

A Balanced Approach for Maximum Outreach

Organic and paid social media strategies are **not competing forces**—they are **complementary tools** that, when used together, create a **powerful digital ministry presence**. By focusing on **authentic engagement, strategic content, and smart advertising investments**, ministries can **reach more people, deepen connections, and drive greater Kingdom impact**.

As the next chapter explores **AI and Web3's role in social media ministry**, ministries must prepare to embrace **cutting-edge tools** while maintaining a **genuine, faith-centered approach**. The future of digital evangelism lies in the balance between **time-tested community building and innovative digital strategies**.

The Role of AI and Web3 in Social Media Ministry

Embracing AI and Web3: The Next Frontier for Digital Ministry

In today's fast-moving digital world, ministries must continually evolve to **reach people where they are**. Social media is no longer just a tool; it's a digital front door for faith communities. Artificial Intelligence (AI) and Web3 technologies are rapidly changing how ministries engage, personalize outreach, and build online communities. These tools, when used effectively, can amplify the reach of the Gospel and create new opportunities for discipleship.

Faith-based organizations that fail to integrate **AI-powered automation** and **Web3 decentralization** into their digital strategies risk falling behind. The challenge is no longer just about having an online presence—it's about using cutting-edge technology to build deep, lasting connections with audiences worldwide. AI and Web3 are not future possibilities; they are **present-day opportunities** to innovate, strengthen engagement, and ensure the Gospel continues to spread.

AI in Social Media Ministry – More Than Just Automation

Artificial Intelligence is transforming social media ministry by enabling churches and faith-based organizations to create, distribute, and optimize content with unprecedented efficiency. Here's how AI enhances faith-based social media outreach:

1. AI-Powered Content Creation

- **Automated Sermon Summaries** – AI tools like Otter.ai and Descript can analyze sermons and generate **social media-ready quotes, blog posts, and short clips** to expand reach.
- **AI-Generated Video Captions** – Platforms like Kapwing or Rev.ai provide **real-time closed captioning**, making sermons and digital content more accessible to global and hearing-impaired audiences.
- **AI Chatbots for Discipleship** – AI chatbots on Facebook Messenger or WhatsApp can provide **24/7 spiritual guidance, prayer requests, and scripture recommendations.**

2. AI-Driven Personalization & Audience Insights

- AI helps ministries understand **which content resonates most** by analyzing **engagement patterns, sentiment analysis, and demographic trends.**

49

- **Personalized devotionals** – AI can recommend Bible readings based on **previous interactions**, tailoring spiritual content for different audience segments.

3. AI for Social Media Strategy & Automation

- **AI-powered scheduling** ensures that posts go live when followers are most active.
- **Content repurposing tools** help ministries **automatically convert long sermons into bite-sized social posts, YouTube shorts, and reels** for wider reach.
- **AI-driven sentiment analysis** helps identify trends in **audience feedback**, allowing ministries to pivot quickly when engagement declines.

Web3 in Ministry – Decentralizing Faith Communities

Web3, built on **blockchain technology**, is changing how ministries handle **ownership, engagement, and digital giving**. Here's why it matters:

1. Decentralized Christian Communities

- Web3 allows ministries to create **blockchain-based digital communities** free from the algorithmic restrictions of major social media platforms.
- Ministries can build **secure, censorship-resistant networks** where believers connect directly **without reliance on Big Tech.**

2. Faith-Based NFTs & Digital Ownership

- Some ministries are **minting NFTs** (Non-Fungible Tokens) as digital collectibles that unlock **exclusive Bible study materials, sermon archives, or online events.**
- NFTs can serve as **fundraising tools**, providing donors with a **unique digital asset** in return for their support.

3. Blockchain-Based Digital Giving

- **Cryptocurrency donations** are becoming an alternative to traditional online giving, allowing ministries to **receive donations globally with lower transaction fees.**
- **Smart contracts** on the blockchain ensure **100% transparency** in how donations are allocated, strengthening donor trust.

4. The Metaverse & Digital Worship Spaces

- Some churches are building **VR-based worship experiences** where believers can attend church in **virtual spaces.**
- Ministries leveraging **decentralized metaverse platforms** can **host global prayer meetings, discipleship classes, and interactive sermon discussions** without geographical barriers.

Balancing Technology with Faith – The Ethics of AI & Web3 in Ministry

While AI and Web3 offer powerful tools, ministries must navigate **ethical concerns** such as:

- **Avoiding AI bias** – Ensuring that AI-driven sermon recommendations **align with sound doctrine** and not just trending topics.
- **Digital Privacy** – Protecting believers' personal data in **Web3 platforms and AI-driven analytics.**

- **Maintaining Authenticity** – AI should **enhance human-led ministry, not replace genuine spiritual interactions.**

Implementation Roadmap – How Ministries Can Start Using AI & Web3

1. Start Small

- Use AI tools like **ChatGPT, Canva AI, or Lumen5** for content creation and automation.
- Integrate **AI-driven engagement tools** to improve response time and audience engagement.

2. Train Your Team

- Educate your social media team on AI-powered analytics and **Web3 fundamentals.**
- Encourage **ethical discussions** on how to balance technology with faith-based values.

3. Experiment with Web3 Giving

- Offer **cryptocurrency donation options** and test blockchain-based transparency models.
- Develop a **community-driven NFT campaign** to fundraise for special ministry projects.

4. Monitor & Adjust

- Use AI-driven engagement insights to **refine content strategy** over time.
- Analyze **Web3 adoption rates** and pivot strategies based on audience response.

The Future of AI and Web3 in Ministry

The digital landscape is evolving faster than ever, and ministries that embrace **AI and Web3** will **stay ahead, expand their reach, and build lasting, decentralized communities.**

This is **not about replacing human connection** but **enhancing engagement with powerful new tools** that allow the Gospel to **reach every corner of the digital world.**

As we move into the next chapter, we'll see **why live streaming is the next essential step for faith-based digital strategy.** Ministries that successfully integrate **AI-powered social engagement** with **Web3-based community building** will **pave the way for a future-proof media presence.**

Lee Allen Miller

4 Streaming: Reaching a Global Audience

Why Live Streaming is Essential for Ministries

The Shift from the Pulpit to the Screen

On any given Sunday, millions of people around the world engage with faith communities—not by stepping into a church building, but by watching a service on their phone, tablet, or smart TV. Some are believers seeking encouragement, others are curious seekers exploring faith for the first time. The shift from in-person-only ministry to digital-first engagement is undeniable, and ministries that fail to recognize this transformation risk fading into irrelevance.

Live streaming is not a trend; it is the new standard. While social media introduced ministries to digital engagement, streaming solidifies ongoing discipleship by providing real-time connection, global reach, and a seamless experience for members and visitors alike. If your church or ministry is not actively streaming, you are leaving the front door of your faith community closed to an entire generation seeking God online.

Digital-First Ministry is the New Normal

The traditional model of church attendance—where someone visits in person as their first introduction to faith—is quickly becoming outdated. Instead, people now encounter ministries through digital platforms first, long before they ever step inside a church building. Studies show that churches that embrace live streaming experience **increased** attendance and engagement, not a decrease.

Live streaming provides an essential on-ramp to faith, offering seekers a safe and familiar way to explore spiritual content. Many individuals who hesitate to enter a church due to fear, past trauma, or uncertainty feel more comfortable engaging with a live stream from their home. By providing access to sermons, worship, and community discussions in real time, churches remove barriers to engagement and create opportunities for long-term discipleship.

Reaching Beyond Four Walls—The Global Church Movement

Live streaming enables ministries to transcend geographical boundaries. A small congregation in rural America can reach believers in Africa, Europe, or Asia. A pastor's message, once confined to a local audience, can now impact thousands across continents with a single broadcast.

Consider the example of a small-town pastor who began streaming Sunday services to accommodate elderly and homebound members. To his surprise, his sermons reached viewers in multiple countries who had never set foot in a church. The global church is no longer limited by location, and ministries that embrace this reality are seeing unprecedented growth.

The Great Commission in the Digital Age

Jesus commanded His followers to *"go and make disciples of all nations"* (Matthew 28:19). In today's media-driven world, live streaming is one of the most powerful ways to fulfill this calling. Just as Paul used letters to communicate with churches across regions, we now use live video to reach people beyond physical borders.

Live streaming is not a replacement for in-person community but an **extension** of the Great Commission. It allows ministries to go where the people are—online. Churches that resist digital transformation are not just resisting technology; they are resisting opportunities for evangelism and outreach.

Community Engagement in Real Time

Unlike pre-recorded content, live streaming creates an interactive, real-time experience. Viewers can engage in live chat, ask for prayer, and participate in worship regardless of location. This two-way engagement makes faith tangible and fosters deep connections that static content cannot replicate.

Examples of ministries using live streaming effectively include:

- Hosting live Q&A sessions where pastors answer questions from viewers.
- Offering real-time prayer support via chat.
- Encouraging online small groups that connect through weekly streamed Bible studies.

Churches that integrate live interaction into their streams build stronger faith communities and keep members engaged beyond Sunday services.

Addressing the Skeptics—Does Streaming Weaken the Church?

Some church leaders worry that streaming services will lead to lower in-person attendance. However, research shows the opposite. Online engagement often serves as a **gateway** to in-person involvement. Many people who begin watching a church online eventually seek deeper connection by attending live events, volunteering, or joining small groups.

Moreover, live streaming reaches those who physically cannot attend—homebound individuals, people in hospitals, missionaries abroad, and those traveling for work. Rather than weakening the church, streaming **expands** its influence and impact.

Is Your Ministry Discoverable?

Imagine a seeker searching online for answers about faith. Will they find your ministry? Or will they only find secular voices filling the digital space?

In today's world, having a church website is not enough. Ministries must be actively present on live streaming platforms, ensuring that when people search for hope, encouragement, and truth, they encounter the Gospel. This is not about chasing trends; it is about making sure that the message of Christ remains visible and accessible in the digital age.

Preparing for the Next Step

Understanding *why* live streaming is essential is only the first step. The next chapter will dive into *how* to create an effective, compelling live streaming experience that maximizes engagement and impact. As you reflect on your ministry's digital presence, consider this:

If someone were searching for hope today, would they find your ministry? Or would they pass by an unopened digital door?

The time to embrace live streaming is now. The world is watching. Is your ministry ready to be seen?

Building a Compelling Streaming Experience

The Role of Streaming in Today's Ministry Landscape

The way people consume content has fundamentally changed. Traditional Sunday services alone are no longer sufficient for maintaining connection and engagement. Streaming provides an opportunity for ministries to:

- **Expand Their Reach** – Livestreaming makes it possible to reach people anywhere in the world, including those who are homebound, traveling, or living in regions without a local church.
- **Increase Engagement Beyond Sunday** – Midweek Bible studies, Q&A sessions, prayer meetings, and behind-the-scenes content can keep your audience engaged throughout the week.
- **Offer On-Demand Spiritual Content** – Viewers can engage with sermons, teachings, and worship sessions at their convenience, ensuring that ministry happens on their schedule.
- **Foster Deeper Connections** – Interactive streaming allows for real-time engagement, creating opportunities for community-building through live chats, virtual prayer rooms, and interactive elements.

Ministries that do not integrate streaming into their outreach strategy risk becoming irrelevant in the digital age. To be effective, faith-based organizations must understand how to build a compelling streaming experience that goes beyond a simple video feed.

Crafting an Engaging Viewing Experience

A successful streaming experience is more than just a camera pointing at a stage. It should be immersive, visually appealing, and structured in a way that retains attention.

1. High-Quality Production Matters

- **Video Quality** – Stream in HD or higher to provide a crisp, clear image. Consider multiple camera angles to make the experience more dynamic.
- **Audio Clarity** – Invest in quality microphones and audio mixing to ensure sermons, music, and discussions are heard clearly.
- **Lighting & Visuals** – Proper lighting highlights speakers and worship teams without harsh shadows. Branded graphics, sermon slides, and overlays enhance the experience.
- **Internet Connection & Reliability** – A stable, high-speed internet connection avoids buffering or dropped streams. A dedicated internet line for streaming is ideal.

2. Structuring the Broadcast for Maximum Engagement

- **Start with an Engaging Hook** – The first 60 seconds are crucial. Welcome viewers, set expectations, and introduce the topic quickly.
- **Keep It Interactive** – Use live chat, polls, and interactive features to keep people engaged throughout the stream.
- **Optimize Sermon Length** – Online attention spans differ from in-person audiences. Consider tightening the message to **25-35 minutes** to maintain engagement.

- **Encourage Participation** – Give clear calls to action, such as inviting viewers to comment, share the stream, or engage with the community.
- **End with a Clear Next Step** – Whether it's joining a small group, attending an event, or supporting the ministry, provide a clear and simple next step for viewers.

Choosing the Right Streaming Platforms

Not all streaming platforms are created equal. Ministries need to strategically choose platforms that best align with their audience and mission.

Top Platforms for Faith-Based Streaming:

- **Facebook Live** – Ideal for reaching large audiences with built-in engagement tools like comments, reactions, and sharing.
- **YouTube Live** – A strong option for ministries wanting high-quality video archives, better search visibility, and the ability to monetize content.
- **Church Online Platform** – Designed specifically for churches, offering interactive features like live prayer requests, sermon notes, and giving options.
- **Roku & Apple TV Apps** – For ministries looking to offer a more professional, dedicated streaming experience through connected TV devices.
- **Custom Websites & Apps** – Building a **dedicated streaming experience** ensures full control over branding, engagement tools, and monctization options.

Multi-Streaming for Maximum Reach

Streaming to multiple platforms at once broadens your audience. Services like Restream and StreamYard allow ministries to broadcast across Facebook, YouTube, and other platforms simultaneously.

Engaging Your Online Audience Like a Congregation

A compelling streaming experience is not a one-way broadcast—it's an opportunity for real-time interaction and community-building.

1. Live Engagement Tactics

- **Moderators & Chat Hosts** – Assign team members to welcome viewers, answer questions, and encourage interaction in the chat.
- **Encourage Viewer Participation** – Ask questions, read comments live, and create moments where viewers can engage (e.g., "Drop an Amen in the chat!").
- **Use Pinned Comments & Links** – Guide viewers to key resources, donation pages, or next steps using pinned comments and on-screen links.

2. Community Beyond the Livestream

- **Create Private Groups** – Facebook Groups, Discord servers, or WhatsApp communities help build deeper relationships beyond the stream.
- **Host Virtual Meetups** – Midweek Bible studies, prayer calls, or Q&A sessions create more touchpoints for connection.
- **Follow-Up Emails & Messages** – Automated email follow-ups thanking viewers and providing next steps can keep them engaged with your ministry.

Monetization & Sustainability for Faith-Based Streaming

While ministry is about outreach, sustainability is key to maintaining a high-quality streaming experience.

1. Digital Giving Strategies

- **Seamless Donation Integration** – Platforms like Church Online or YouTube Super Chat make it easy for viewers to give directly during the stream.
- **On-Screen Giving Reminders** – A simple on-screen prompt or QR code makes tithing frictionless.
- **Encourage Viewers to Support the Mission** – Frame giving as an opportunity to participate in expanding the reach of the Gospel.

2. Subscription & Premium Content

- **Exclusive Content for Supporters** – Offering premium Bible studies, leadership training, or exclusive Q&A sessions can create a sustainable revenue model.
- **Membership-Based Streaming** – Platforms like Patreon or custom ministry apps can offer deeper engagement opportunities for monthly supporters.

Key Takeaways

- **Faith-based streaming is essential** for reaching new audiences and engaging beyond Sunday services.
- **Production quality matters**—audio, video, lighting, and internet stability all impact viewer retention.
- **Interaction is key**—engage with your audience in real-time to build an online faith community.
- **Multi-platform strategy maximizes reach**—consider streaming across Facebook, YouTube, and dedicated church platforms.

- **Sustainability matters**—integrating digital giving and premium content can fund your streaming efforts long-term.

Next Chapter Preview

The next chapter will focus on **Monetization & Funding Strategies for Faith-Based Streaming**, exploring sustainable ways to fund and expand digital outreach.

Monetization & Funding Strategies for Faith-Based Streaming

The Challenge of Funding Digital Ministry

As faith-based organizations expand into the digital realm, one major challenge consistently arises—how to sustain and fund online ministry effectively. While live streaming and digital content offer unprecedented reach, many ministries struggle to cover the operational costs, technology upgrades, and staff needed to maintain high-quality productions. Without a clear monetization strategy, even the most compelling content can become financially unsustainable.

Some ministries hesitate to discuss monetization, fearing it may appear as prioritizing profit over the message. However, the reality is that effective outreach requires resources. Just as traditional churches rely on tithes and offerings to operate, digital ministries need sustainable funding models. In this chapter, we will explore how faith-based streaming can be monetized ethically and effectively without compromising mission or integrity.

The Biblical Perspective on Monetization

Balancing ministry and financial stewardship is not a new challenge. Throughout scripture, we see examples of faithful leaders ensuring that resources were available for God's work.

- **Paul's Tentmaking Model:** The apostle Paul worked as a tentmaker to support his ministry (Acts 18:3). His approach illustrates that ministry and financial sustainability can go hand in hand.
- **The Early Church's Community Model:** The early church was funded through generous giving, where believers pooled their resources to support those in need (Acts 2:44-45).
- **Jesus and Financial Support:** Even Jesus' ministry was financially supported by donors, including women who provided for Him and His disciples (Luke 8:1-3).

The lesson? Sustainable funding is not unspiritual—it is essential to long-term ministry effectiveness. When done with transparency and integrity, monetization enables ministries to extend their reach, invest in high-quality content, and serve their communities more effectively.

Traditional Funding Models for Streaming Ministries

Faith-based streaming ministries often rely on traditional funding models, many of which have been successful for churches and nonprofit organizations for decades.

Tithes & Offerings for Digital Ministries

For ministries with an existing congregation, encouraging digital tithing can be a game-changer. Platforms like **Tithe.ly, Pushpay,** and **Givelify** allow churches to receive offerings digitally, making it easy for online audiences to support their mission.

Implementation Tip: Set up an easy-to-use donation page on your website and remind viewers during live streams how they can give.

Donor Campaigns & Crowdfunding

Nonprofit ministries often use fundraising campaigns and crowdfunding to finance specific projects. Platforms like **GoFundMe, GiveSendGo,** and **Fundly** allow faith-based organizations to reach a wider audience beyond their immediate congregation.

Case Study: A small ministry in Texas launched a **GoFundMe** campaign to upgrade their live-streaming equipment. By explaining the impact their content had on viewers and sharing testimonies, they exceeded their fundraising goal in just two months.

Grants & Partnerships

Many Christian organizations and foundations offer grants specifically for media outreach and digital evangelism. Partnering with mission-aligned sponsors or denominational networks can provide additional funding opportunities.

Action Step: Research and apply for grants from organizations like **Lilly Endowment, The Mustard Seed Foundation,** or **NRB (National Religious Broadcasters).**

Modern Revenue Streams for Faith-Based Streaming

While traditional models are foundational, modern revenue strategies have emerged as viable funding options for faith-based streaming ministries.

Subscription Models & Private Memberships

Platforms like **Patreon, Substack,** and **Locals** allow ministries to offer premium content to dedicated supporters in exchange for a monthly subscription.

Example: A ministry that produces in-depth Bible study videos could offer exclusive access to deeper teachings, Q&A sessions, and behind-the-scenes content for $10/month.

YouTube Monetization & Social Media Funding

If your ministry has a substantial online following, social media monetization can be an effective revenue stream.

- **YouTube Partner Program:** Earn ad revenue, receive "Super Chats" during live streams, and offer paid memberships.
- **Facebook Stars:** Viewers can send virtual stars that convert into real money.
- **TikTok & Instagram Creator Funds:** Short-form content can generate income based on views and engagement.

Pro Tip: Ministries should be cautious with ad-based monetization to ensure that ads align with their values.

Sponsorships & Corporate Partnerships

Working with mission-aligned businesses or organizations can be a win-win strategy. Brands looking to support faith-based initiatives may sponsor content, provide funding, or offer affiliate partnerships.

Example: A Christian apparel company might sponsor a ministry's weekly podcast, providing financial support in exchange for product mentions.

The Rise of Web3 & Blockchain in Ministry Funding

Emerging technologies like Web3 and blockchain are changing the way donations and digital ownership work in ministry.

Cryptocurrency Donations

Ministries can now accept **Bitcoin, Ethereum,** and other cryptocurrencies as donations through platforms like **Engiven** and **The Giving Block.**

Why it matters: Crypto donations offer tax advantages for donors and can attract a new generation of digital-savvy givers.

NFTs & Digital Ownership

Non-fungible tokens (NFTs) can be used creatively in ministry fundraising. Churches or ministries can sell digital artwork, exclusive sermon recordings, or special access to community events as NFTs.

Example: A Christian artist partnered with a ministry to sell NFT-based worship album downloads, raising funds for their outreach programs.

Practical Steps to Implement a Monetization Plan

Step 1: Define Your Ministry's Financial Goals

- What are your short-term and long-term funding needs?
- How much does it cost to maintain and grow your streaming platform?

Step 2: Choose Multiple Revenue Streams

Diversification is key—combine traditional funding (donations, grants) with modern strategies (subscriptions, social media monetization).

Step 3: Be Transparent & Communicate Value

- Regularly update supporters on how their contributions are being used.
- Share impact stories and testimonials.

Step 4: Create a Call-to-Action Strategy

- Encourage donations during live streams.
- Use end screens and pinned comments on YouTube.
- Make giving simple and seamless on your website.

Step 5: Monitor & Adjust

Use analytics to track the effectiveness of each monetization strategy and adjust based on audience engagement and response.

Funding Ministry with Faith and Strategy

Monetization isn't about selling the Gospel—it's about sustaining and expanding the reach of faith-based content. By combining biblical principles, traditional funding models, and modern revenue strategies, ministries can build a sustainable streaming presence that glorifies God and serves their audience effectively.

With careful planning, transparency, and a heart for impact, faith-based organizations can not only survive in the digital age but thrive in ways that allow them to reach more people with the message of Christ than ever before.

Lee Allen Miller

5 Broadcast & Cable: The Power of Legacy Media

The Enduring Influence of Television & Radio

Why TV & Radio Still Matter in Faith-Based Media

Despite the rapid rise of digital media, television and radio continue to hold a significant place in faith-based outreach. While streaming and social media provide immediacy and interactive engagement, traditional broadcast platforms remain essential for reaching key demographics, maintaining credibility, and expanding the reach of ministries. Understanding the unique strengths of TV and radio is crucial for ministries that seek to build a multi-platform strategy rather than abandoning traditional media altogether.

Television's Power of Visual Storytelling

Television has long been the gold standard for visual storytelling. For faith-based organizations, it provides an unparalleled medium to share sermons, interviews, testimonials, and worship experiences with high production value. The ability to combine powerful imagery, music, and spoken word makes television a dynamic tool for inspiration and education. Moreover, TV broadcasts carry a level of legitimacy and authority that digital platforms often struggle to match. Viewers tend to associate television with well-established brands and trustworthiness, making it an ideal medium for delivering the Gospel message.

Faith-based television networks such as TBN, Daystar, and CBN have capitalized on this enduring trust. These networks provide a structured and consistent platform for ministries to reach audiences who still rely on television as their primary source of faith-based content. Even local churches that partner with regional broadcast stations can experience increased visibility and credibility.

Radio's Accessibility and Connection

Radio remains a vital tool for ministries, particularly in reaching audiences who may not have reliable internet access. Unlike television and social media, which require dedicated attention, radio is a companion medium—people listen while commuting, working, or engaging in daily activities. This passive yet consistent engagement fosters a deep connection between ministries and their audiences.

Christian radio networks such as K-LOVE, Moody Radio, and Bott Radio Network have demonstrated that audio content remains a powerful force for faith-based communication. Sermons, devotionals, and Christian music provide daily encouragement and guidance to millions of listeners. Unlike social media, where content is fleeting, radio programs have a structured format that ensures consistent engagement.

Additionally, radio is often the first point of access to faith-based content for incarcerated individuals, hospital patients, and those in rural areas. Many ministries use radio as a cost-effective way to reach souls who might never step foot in a church or access digital platforms.

The Role of Legacy Media in a Multi-Platform Strategy

Rather than viewing television and radio as outdated, ministries should integrate these legacy platforms into a broader digital-first strategy. By understanding the unique strengths of each medium, faith-based organizations can create a unified outreach model that maximizes their impact.

1. **Television Drives Digital Engagement**: TV programs can be repurposed into short clips for social media, podcasts, and YouTube channels. Ministries should promote website links and mobile apps during broadcasts to encourage audience migration to digital platforms.

2. **Radio Builds Trust and Loyalty**: A strong presence in radio helps solidify a ministry's reputation. Live call-in shows, listener testimonials, and syndicated sermons can all serve as a bridge between traditional and digital audiences.

3. **Cross-Promotion Strengthens Engagement**: Ministries can use their digital platforms to promote upcoming TV specials and radio broadcasts. Likewise, on-air promotions can drive traffic to social media, email lists, and livestream services.

How Faith-Based Broadcasters Can Maximize Their Impact

For television and radio to remain effective, ministries must embrace modern best practices:

- **Invest in High-Quality Production**: Today's audiences expect professional visuals and sound. Ministries should work with experienced media teams to enhance the quality of their broadcasts.

- **Compelling Storytelling**: Avoid overly formal presentations. Engage audiences with personal testimonies, interactive segments, and behind-the-scenes content.

- **Leverage Viewer & Listener Feedback**: Audience insights from calls, letters, emails, and social media comments can guide content strategies.

- **Diversify Distribution Channels**: Ensure that TV sermons are available on-demand via YouTube, ministry websites, and podcasts. Similarly, radio programs should be repurposed into streaming audio content.

Case Studies: Ministries Thriving on TV & Radio

- **Joel Osteen's Television Ministry**: Lakewood Church continues to thrive through its weekly TV broadcasts, reaching millions worldwide. By integrating streaming and social media, Osteen's ministry successfully bridges traditional and digital audiences.

- **Focus on the Family Radio Broadcast**: This long-running program remains a staple in Christian households. Its ability to tackle contemporary issues while maintaining a faith-based approach keeps listeners engaged.

- **Elevation Church's Multichannel Strategy**: Pastor Steven Furtick uses both TV and YouTube to amplify his sermons. By utilizing polished production and timely messages, his ministry captures audiences across different platforms.

The Future of TV & Radio in Faith-Based Media

The evolution of media does not mean the demise of television and radio—it means adaptation. Faith-based broadcasters must embrace emerging technologies to stay relevant:

- **Hybrid TV & Streaming Models**: Many Christian TV networks are launching their own apps and on-demand services to meet the needs of digital audiences.

- **Podcasting as an Extension of Radio**: Many successful radio ministries are repurposing their content into podcast formats to attract younger listeners.

- **Smart TV & Connected Devices**: Ministries should ensure their broadcasts are accessible on Roku, Apple TV, and other smart TV platforms to reach a tech-savvy audience.

Legacy Media as a Pillar of Outreach

Television and radio are far from obsolete. While digital media continues to evolve, legacy broadcast platforms remain powerful tools for faith-based outreach. Ministries that strategically blend

TV, radio, streaming, and social media will create an enduring and impactful presence.

Rather than abandoning traditional media, ministries must innovate within it. By doing so, they can reach audiences across generations, ensuring that the Gospel message continues to thrive in an ever-changing media landscape. Now is not the time to retreat from television and radio—it's the time to redefine their role in a powerful, unified media strategy.

Adapting Traditional Broadcast to a Digital-First World

Introduction: The Evolution of Traditional Broadcast Media

For decades, television and radio have been cornerstones of faith-based outreach. They've reached millions, provided spiritual nourishment, and built strong communities of believers. But in today's digital-first world, the way audiences consume media has shifted drastically. Ministries that once relied solely on broadcast must now navigate an ecosystem where on-demand content, social media, and streaming platforms dominate.

Traditional broadcast isn't dying—it's evolving. Faith-based media leaders must understand how to integrate their well-established television and radio presence into a strategy that prioritizes digital engagement. By embracing modern distribution methods while preserving the impact of legacy media, ministries can remain relevant and expand their reach like never before.

This chapter will explore how ministries can adapt traditional broadcast to thrive in today's digital-first world. We'll uncover practical strategies to bridge the gap between legacy media and new digital platforms, ensuring that ministries maximize their outreach potential.

The Shifting Media Landscape: Why Ministries Must Adapt

From Scheduled to On-Demand Consumption

For yoarc, faith-based programming followed a predictable model: a church service or teaching segment aired at a set time on a local or national broadcast channel. Viewers tuned in, watched, and often planned their schedules around these programs.

Today, audiences expect content to be available *whenever* and *wherever* they want. The rise of streaming services like YouTube, Roku, Apple TV, and social media platforms has conditioned viewers to demand flexibility. Faith-based media must meet people where they are, offering content in formats that fit their daily lives.

Declining Cable Subscriptions & The Rise of OTT

Cord-cutting is accelerating. Over-the-top (OTT) streaming services—content delivered over the internet without requiring traditional cable or satellite—are now preferred by younger audiences and growing segments of older viewers alike. Faith-based networks and ministries must recognize that while traditional television still has value, a significant portion of their audience may no longer have access to it.

Ministries must distribute their content across multiple platforms, including their own branded apps, YouTube, Facebook Live, and emerging OTT services. This shift requires a mindset change— from simply *broadcasting* to strategically *distributing* content across various digital and traditional channels.

Audience Behavior: Engagement Over Passive Viewing

Traditional television and radio were one-way communication tools. Ministries delivered their messages, and audiences passively consumed them. Today's digital-first world demands engagement. Viewers expect interaction, real-time responses, and opportunities to participate in conversations.

To thrive in a digital-first world, faith-based broadcasters must create opportunities for engagement. This means integrating chat features into live streams, responding to comments on social media, and offering exclusive behind-the-scenes content to keep audiences connected.

Bridging the Gap Between Traditional Broadcast and Digital Platforms

1. Simulcasting: The Easy First Step

One of the simplest ways for ministries to transition into the digital-first era is by simulcasting their television and radio broadcasts on digital platforms. This means airing the same content live on multiple platforms simultaneously, including:

- **YouTube Live**
- **Facebook Live**
- **Ministry Websites**
- **Church Apps**
- **Roku, Apple TV, and Amazon Fire TV**

Simulcasting allows ministries to maintain their traditional audience while expanding their reach to digital viewers. More importantly, it provides an easy entry point into the world of digital distribution without requiring significant changes to existing workflows.

2. On-Demand Libraries: Giving Viewers Control

Traditional broadcast schedules don't work for everyone. Some audiences can't watch live, while others may want to revisit content at their convenience. Creating an on-demand content library allows ministries to serve their audiences on their own terms.

Steps to Build an On-Demand Library:

- Upload past sermons and programs to **YouTube** and **Facebook Video**

- Offer a categorized **video archive** on the ministry's website

- Develop a **mobile app** with easy access to past episodes

- Partner with **faith-based streaming services** to reach OTT audiences

By allowing viewers to access faith-based content whenever they choose, ministries increase engagement and extend the lifespan of their messages.

3. Repurposing Content Across Multiple Platforms

Content repurposing ensures that a single sermon or program reaches audiences in multiple formats. A one-hour TV program can be transformed into:

- **Short-form videos** (ideal for TikTok, Instagram Reels, and YouTube Shorts)

- **Podcast episodes** (extracted audio available on Spotify and Apple Podcasts)

- **Blog posts** (summarizing key points with scripture references)

- **Email newsletters** (featuring highlights and viewer testimonies)

- **Social media graphics** (sharing key takeaways)

Repurposing content amplifies reach and ensures that messages resonate across all platforms, not just traditional TV and radio.

Building a Sustainable Broadcast-to-Digital Transition Strategy

1. Rethink Content Distribution

A modern faith-based media strategy must distribute content intentionally. Ministries should adopt a **platform-first** mindset:

- **Live content goes to:** Broadcast TV, radio, Facebook Live, YouTube Live

- **On-demand content goes to:** YouTube, podcast platforms, ministry websites

- **Short-form content goes to:** Instagram, TikTok, Twitter, email campaigns

Creating a roadmap for content distribution ensures that no message is limited to just one channel.

2. Monetization: Funding Broadcast & Digital Growth

Transitioning from traditional broadcast to digital requires financial investment. Ministries should explore new monetization strategies, including:

- **YouTube ad revenue** (monetizing views with YouTube Partner Program)

- **Sponsorships & partnerships** (faith-based brands supporting content)

- **Subscription-based apps** (offering exclusive content for members)

- **Crowdfunding & donations** (engaging audiences to support digital expansion)

- **Syndication & licensing** (offering content to multiple broadcasters)

A strong monetization plan allows ministries to scale their digital presence while maintaining financial sustainability.

3. Training and Team Building

Many traditional broadcast teams lack experience in digital media. Ministries should invest in training their staff on:

- **SEO & YouTube growth strategies**

- **Social media engagement techniques**

- **Live streaming best practices**

- **Content analytics & data interpretation**

By equipping teams with digital-first skills, ministries ensure a seamless transition into modern media strategies.

Embracing the Future: What's Next for Faith-Based Media?

The transition from traditional broadcast to a digital-first world isn't just a trend—it's an urgent necessity. Ministries that fail to adapt risk losing relevance, while those that embrace change will see exponential growth in audience engagement and outreach impact.

The Future of Faith-Based Media Includes:

- **AI-driven content personalization** (delivering tailored messages based on viewer preferences)

- **Virtual & Augmented Reality Church Experiences** (immersive faith-based content)

- **Interactive Live Streams** (real-time Q&As, prayer sessions, and community discussions)

- **Blockchain-based Faith Networks** (secure donation systems and community engagement tools)

As technology continues to advance, ministries must stay ahead by exploring new ways to integrate digital tools into their outreach strategies.

Key Takeaways

- Traditional broadcast media is still powerful but must be integrated with digital strategies.
- Simulcasting, on-demand libraries, and content repurposing extend audience reach

- Faith-based organizations must rethink content distribution and diversify monetization.
- Training teams in digital media skills is essential for long-term success.
- The future of faith-based media will include AI, VR, and blockchain-driven engagement.

The call is clear: adapt or fade. The future of faith-based media belongs to those who embrace both **legacy influence** and **digital-first innovation.** Ministries that master this balance will build an outreach powerhouse that spans generations and transforms lives worldwide.

Syndication, Partnerships, and Distribution Strategies

The Power of Syndication: Expanding Your Reach Beyond Boundaries

Syndication is one of the most powerful tools for ministries and faith-based organizations looking to maximize their impact. In its simplest form, syndication allows content—whether sermons, talk shows, or faith-based documentaries—to be distributed across multiple platforms and networks. This strategy enables organizations to extend their reach far beyond their local congregation or primary audience.

The concept of syndication is well-established in traditional media. For example, a successful TV ministry can take a sermon recorded at a local church and distribute it across multiple networks, cable channels, and even streaming services. Instead of being limited to a single airtime on one network, that same sermon can air in different time slots across various networks, reaching different audiences.

But syndication is no longer just for TV and radio. The rise of digital platforms means ministries can now syndicate their content across YouTube, Facebook Watch, podcast networks, and faith-based streaming services like PureFlix or RightNow Media.

How to Build a Syndication Strategy

1. **Content Optimization:** Ensure that your content is formatted for multiple platforms. This might mean re-editing TV broadcasts into shorter social media clips or converting sermons into podcast episodes.

2. **Distribution Partners:** Identify platforms, networks, and organizations that align with your mission. Faith-based networks, community television stations, and even international broadcasters may be interested in carrying your programming.

3. **Multi-Format Availability:** Syndicate content across different formats—video, audio, written transcripts—so that audiences can engage in their preferred way.

4. **Licensing Agreements:** Establish clear agreements with syndication partners about rights, revenue sharing (if applicable), and scheduling. Ministries should retain ownership of their content while maximizing its distribution potential.

5. **Data Tracking:** Use analytics to measure engagement across different platforms. Understanding which distribution channels generate the most impact will help refine your syndication strategy over time.

Partnerships: Leveraging Strategic Alliances for Greater Impact

Partnerships allow faith-based content creators to extend their reach by collaborating with organizations that have established audiences. Whether it's working with Christian television networks, collaborating with influencers in the faith-based space, or forming alliances with like-minded ministries, partnerships can exponentially increase visibility.

Types of Strategic Partnerships

- **Media Network Partnerships:** Collaborate with faith-based TV and radio networks to feature your content in their programming lineup.

- **Church Collaborations:** Offer content-sharing agreements where multiple churches can feature the same sermon series across different locations and platforms.

- **Influencer & Content Creator Collaborations:** Work with Christian influencers on YouTube, Instagram, and TikTok to distribute sermon clips, testimonies, and devotional content.

- **Denominational Alliances:** Ministries within the same denomination can create shared resources, expanding their reach across different congregations and communities.

- **Faith-Based Streaming Platforms:** Submit content for inclusion on platforms like RightNow Media, PureFlix, or The Chosen's app.

- **Corporate Sponsorships & Nonprofit Collaborations:** Align with Christian nonprofits, universities, or mission-based organizations that can integrate your content into their outreach efforts.

Distribution Strategies: Placing Your Content Where It Matters

Effective distribution means ensuring that your message reaches your audience at the right time, in the right place, and in the right format. This requires a well-thought-out strategy that takes advantage of multiple distribution channels.

Key Distribution Methods

1. **Broadcast & Cable Distribution:**

   o **National & Local TV Networks:** Seek airtime on Christian television networks such as TBN, Daystar, and The Word Network.

   o **Public Access Channels:** Many local stations allow churches and ministries to air content at little to no cost.

   o **Satellite Broadcasts:** International networks such as GOD TV and CBN provide opportunities for ministries to reach global audiences.

2. **Streaming & Digital Media:**

   o **Social Media Video Distribution:** Facebook, YouTube, Instagram, and TikTok are all powerful platforms where ministries can publish video content.

- o **YouTube Playlists & Premieres:** Creating YouTube series or organizing live premieres can build an engaged audience.

- o **OTT (Over-the-Top) Streaming:** Publish content on faith-based streaming platforms such as Roku channels, Apple TV, or Amazon Fire TV.

- o **Podcast Distribution:** Repurpose sermons and teachings into podcast episodes, making them available on platforms like Spotify, Apple Podcasts, and Google Podcasts.

3. **Sermon Archives & On-Demand Services:**

- o **Church Websites & Mobile Apps:** Many churches have dedicated sermon archives on their websites or church apps where people can watch on demand.

- o **Ministry Email & SMS Distribution:** Sending sermon links via email or SMS can directly connect with an audience that may not always check social media.

4. **International Expansion:**

- o **Language Translation & Subtitles:** Translating sermons into Spanish, Portuguese, Chinese, or other widely spoken languages can open up new global audiences.

- o **Mission Broadcasting:** Work with international faith-based networks to bring content to audiences in regions with limited church access.

    o **YouTube Auto-Translate:** Enable auto-generated subtitles in different languages to make sermons accessible to global viewers.

The Future of Faith-Based Syndication & Distribution

Faith-based media distribution is rapidly evolving. With AI, blockchain, and Web3 developments, ministries will soon have new ways to distribute and monetize their content. **Tokenized content ownership, decentralized broadcasting, and personalized AI-generated devotional content** are just a few of the emerging trends. Ministries that embrace these innovations early will be positioned for long-term sustainability.

Key Takeaways for Ministries Looking to Expand Distribution

- **Think Beyond One Platform:** If your content is only on YouTube or Facebook, you're missing out on a vast audience that consumes media through streaming services, podcasts, and traditional television.

- **Maximize Existing Content:** Repurpose sermons, interviews, and ministry updates into multiple formats for different platforms.

- **Build Relationships with Media Partners:** Collaborating with networks, influencers, and churches expands your distribution potential.

- **Leverage Data for Smarter Distribution:** Use analytics tools to determine which platforms generate the most engagement and optimize accordingly.

- **Prepare for the Future:** Emerging technologies like AI, blockchain, and Web3 will continue to revolutionize content distribution.

By adopting a comprehensive syndication, partnership, and distribution strategy, faith-based media leaders can ensure their message reaches the widest possible audience—both today and in the future. The key is to remain adaptable, stay ahead of technological trends, and embrace the vast opportunities that digital and broadcast media provide.

Lee Allen Miller

6 The Content Ecosystem: Creating and Repurposing for Maximum Impact

Repurposing Content Across Platforms

The Power of Multi-Channel Ministry

Imagine spending hours crafting a powerful sermon, hosting an insightful interview, or producing a compelling television broadcast—only for it to be experienced once and forgotten. Ministries and faith-based organizations often invest tremendous resources into content creation, yet many fail to extend its lifespan beyond the initial release. In today's multi-platform digital landscape, **repurposing content is the key to maximizing impact, reaching new audiences, and increasing engagement across social, streaming, broadcast, and cable.**

This chapter explores **how ministries can strategically repurpose content** to expand their reach while maintaining authenticity and consistency. With practical steps and real-world examples, we'll uncover how to transform a single piece of content into a powerful ecosystem of engagement across multiple channels.

Why Repurposing Content is Essential

1. Reach More People With the Same Message

Not all audiences consume content the same way. Some prefer watching sermons live, others engage with short clips on social media, and many enjoy listening to podcasts while commuting. Repurposing ensures that **your message meets people where they are.**

2. Maximize Your Efforts

Instead of constantly creating new content from scratch, repurposing allows you to **multiply your existing content's value** by adapting it for different platforms.

3. Strengthen Brand Recognition and Message Consistency

When your content is shared across multiple platforms in different formats, it reinforces your ministry's **core message and vision**, increasing familiarity and trust among your audience.

4. Improve Engagement and Community Interaction

A repurposed sermon or podcast clip on Instagram can spark conversations in the comments. A blog post inspired by a Sunday sermon can invite deeper reflection. Repurposing creates **opportunities for ongoing engagement** and discipleship.

The Repurposing Content Framework

Step 1: Identify Your Core Content

Start by identifying **high-value content** that can be adapted for multiple platforms. This may include:

- Weekly sermons or Bible studies
- Interviews with thought leaders
- Testimonies and testimonials
- Conference sessions or workshops
- Behind-the-scenes ministry moments

Step 2: Break It Down Into Multiple Formats

Take your core content and adapt it into **bite-sized pieces** that suit different platforms. Here's how:

- **Video Clips:** Extract impactful moments from a sermon or interview and post them as Reels, Shorts, or TikToks.
- **Blog Posts:** Transform a sermon into a written devotional or a "Key Takeaways" blog post.
- **Podcasts:** Convert long-form content into a podcast episode for on-the-go engagement.
- **Email Series:** Break down key teachings into a week-long email devotional.
- **Social Media Graphics:** Turn key quotes into shareable graphics for Instagram, Facebook, and Twitter.

Step 3: Tailor Content for Each Platform

Each platform has unique requirements and audience behaviors. Customize your content accordingly:

- **YouTube**: Full-length sermons, interviews, or deep-dive explainer videos.

- **Instagram & TikTok**: Short, engaging clips under 60 seconds with captions.

- **Facebook**: Mid-length videos, community discussions, and behind-the-scenes content.

- **Twitter/X**: Threaded conversations, key takeaways, and quick engagement.

- **LinkedIn**: Professional insights, leadership articles, and industry discussions.

- **Email Newsletters**: Exclusive reflections, upcoming events, and direct communication with your audience.

Step 4: Use Automation & AI for Efficiency

Repurposing doesn't mean doing everything manually. Leverage AI and automation tools to streamline the process:

- **Transcription Tools**: Use AI-powered transcribers (Otter.ai, Descript) to quickly turn sermons into blog posts.

- **Automated Video Clipping**: Tools like Canva, InShot, or Kapwing help extract and format video highlights.

- **Social Media Schedulers**: Platforms like Buffer and Hootsuite automate posting across multiple channels.

Case Study: A Church That Multiplied Its Content Reach

Grace Community Church was struggling to maintain its online presence. Every Sunday, they live-streamed their sermons, but engagement was low outside of service times. By implementing a **content repurposing strategy**, they experienced a transformation:

1. **Full Sermon (YouTube & Podcast)** – The full-length video was uploaded to YouTube and an audio version released as a podcast.

2. **Short Clips (Instagram & TikTok)** – Engaging 60-second clips were extracted and shared daily.

3. **Blog Summary (Website & Email)** – A written version of the sermon was emailed to subscribers and posted on their blog.

4. **Key Quotes (Social Media Graphics)** – Eye-catching graphics were created with the sermon's most impactful statements.

Results:

- **YouTube subscribers grew by 40% in three months.**

- **Instagram engagement tripled with short-form video content.**

- **Website traffic increased as more people read sermon recaps.**

- **Podcast downloads surged as on-the-go listeners engaged with the message.**

By **repurposing content efficiently**, Grace Community Church **expanded its reach, increased engagement, and reinforced its core message across all platforms.**

Quick Wins: Start Repurposing Today

Action Step 1: Take your last sermon or teaching and break it into 3 social media clips, 1 blog post, and 1 YouTube Shorts video.

Action Step 2: Use a transcription tool to turn a video into a written article.

Action Step 3: Schedule repurposed content across different platforms for the next two weeks using a content calendar.

Repurposing content isn't just a marketing strategy—it's a **multiplication strategy for ministry.** By adapting messages across platforms, faith-based organizations can **reach more people, deepen engagement, and create a lasting impact**.

Instead of constantly chasing new content, focus on maximizing what you already have. With **a structured approach and the right tools**, your ministry can thrive across social, streaming, broadcast, and cable—ensuring that **no message is wasted, and every platform is used for Kingdom impact.**

Strategies for Maintaining Consistency & Quality

Why Consistency Matters in Faith-Based Media

In an era of digital saturation, maintaining a consistent and high-quality presence across media platforms is essential for faith-based organizations. Whether it's a church, ministry, or faith-driven broadcaster, consistency in messaging and production ensures that audiences recognize and trust your content. Without it, ministries risk confusion, disengagement, and diluted impact.

Consistency in media goes beyond just repeating the same messages—it creates a unified experience for the audience, ensuring that whether someone encounters your content on social media, a live stream, or a broadcast channel, the core values and message remain intact.

Defining Content Standards

Faith-based media must uphold both theological accuracy and brand integrity. Establishing clear content standards allows teams to maintain unity in messaging and prevents miscommunication or misalignment with core beliefs.

Develop a Brand Style Guide

- **Tone and Voice:** Define the voice of your ministry— whether it's formal, conversational, or storytelling-driven.

- **Visual Identity:** Ensure logos, fonts, color palettes, and graphics remain consistent across platforms.

- **Formatting Guidelines:** Standardize how content is structured (e.g., sermon recaps, devotionals, video intros).

Theological and Doctrinal Alignment

- Ensure that all messages align with the church's or ministry's doctrine.

- Implement a review process where leaders or theologians check content for biblical accuracy before release.

- Avoid vague or controversial statements that may create confusion among the audience.

Cultural Relevance and Sensitivity

- Maintain a balance between timeless biblical truths and modern applications.

- Ensure culturally sensitive and inclusive language without compromising biblical integrity.

- Test content with focus groups or advisory boards to gauge potential audience reception.

Maintaining Quality Across Platforms

Ensuring high production value is crucial, regardless of the platform. Quality enhances credibility and engagement while reducing distractions that could take away from the message.

Technical Best Practices

- **Video Production:** Maintain high-resolution formats, proper lighting, and clear audio.

- **Audio Production:** Use noise reduction techniques and high-quality microphones for podcasts and live streams.

- **Writing & Editing:** Implement grammar and style checks to ensure clarity in written content.

Balancing Professionalism with Authenticity

While polished content is necessary, overproducing can sometimes feel impersonal. Ministries should find the balance between excellence and approachability.

- Allow space for organic moments, such as unscripted prayers or testimonies.

- Ensure presenters and speakers maintain natural delivery styles rather than sounding overly rehearsed.

AI & Automation Tools for Quality Control

Leverage AI-driven tools for proofreading, content formatting, and quality assessment. Tools such as Grammarly, Descript, and AI video editors can help maintain a high standard with minimal human error.

Content Planning for Consistency

An effective content strategy involves planning well in advance to ensure alignment across all platforms.

Editorial Calendars

- Create a monthly or quarterly editorial calendar that outlines key themes, scripture references, and target audiences.

- Use cloud-based collaboration tools (e.g., Trello, Asana) to keep team members aligned.

- Designate team leads for each type of content (social media, live streams, devotionals, etc.).

Repurposing Content for Multi-Platform Engagement

- Turn **sermon recordings** into blog posts, podcast episodes, or YouTube clips.

- Break down **long-form content** into bite-sized social media posts (e.g., Twitter threads, Instagram reels).

- Convert **testimonials and Q&A sessions** into shareable content for engagement.

Evergreen vs. Time-Sensitive Content

- **Evergreen Content:** Timeless messages that can be used repeatedly (e.g., salvation messages, faith testimonies).

- **Time-Sensitive Content:** Content tied to seasons, current events, or sermon series.

- Maintain a library of evergreen content to fill gaps in your content calendar when needed.

Leveraging Technology for Consistency & Quality

Technology plays a crucial role in ensuring that content remains cohesive across platforms.

Digital Asset Management (DAM) Systems

- Use centralized cloud storage for images, templates, and video clips to maintain brand consistency.

- Provide team members with access to standardized content resources.

Ensuring Cross-Platform Accessibility

- Include captions and transcripts for video and audio content to increase accessibility.

- Optimize content for multiple devices (mobile, tablet, desktop).

- Offer translations or multilingual content for global outreach.

Training Teams to Uphold Standards

Faith-based media teams are often composed of volunteers and part-time contributors, making training essential for maintaining quality.

Establish Internal Workflows

- Define clear approval processes for content publication.

- Create training materials or onboarding guides for new team members.

Training Volunteer and Media Teams

- Offer workshops on video production, social media management, and storytelling.

- Encourage mentorship between experienced media team members and new recruits.

- Provide ongoing feedback and constructive criticism to refine skills.

Case Study: A Ministry That Maintains High Content Standards

Highlight a real-life example of a church or ministry that successfully balances consistency and quality across multiple platforms. Discuss the strategies they use and how they've built an engaged audience.

Balancing Innovation with Consistency

While maintaining consistency is essential, faith-based media organizations should remain adaptable to emerging platforms and technologies.

Adapting to New Platforms

- Experiment with new formats like TikTok evangelism, AI chatbots for Q&A, or virtual reality church experiences.

- Ensure that all new platform content aligns with your brand's core message and theology.

Experimenting with New Content Formats

- Leverage interactive media (live Q&A, polls, and community discussions) to engage audiences.

- Introduce podcasting or vlogging if it complements your existing strategy.

Future-Proofing Faith-Based Media Content

- Stay ahead of trends in digital ministry without compromising core values.

- Build a content archive that can be adapted as technology evolves.

- Engage younger generations by incorporating innovative storytelling methods.

Maintaining consistency and quality in faith-based media is about more than aesthetics—it's about reinforcing a trustworthy and impactful presence that serves audiences effectively. By implementing structured workflows, leveraging technology, and training teams to uphold high standards, ministries can ensure that their message remains powerful, clear, and engaging across all platforms. As the digital landscape continues to evolve, faith-based media leaders must strike the right balance between consistency and innovation, ensuring that their content remains relevant while staying true to their mission.

Building a Sustainable Production Workflow

The Foundation of a Sustainable Content Workflow

In today's digital landscape, ministries and faith-based media organizations must maintain a steady flow of high-quality content to engage their audience effectively. However, without a structured workflow, content creation can become overwhelming, leading to burnout and inconsistency. A sustainable production workflow ensures efficiency, maintains quality, and aligns with the ministry's mission—all while being scalable and cost-effective.

This chapter explores how to build a production workflow that optimizes resources, integrates modern technology, and fosters collaboration, ensuring long-term success in media outreach.

The Three Pillars of a Scalable Production System

1. Pre-Production: Planning with Purpose

A well-organized pre-production process is crucial to minimizing stress and maximizing content impact. Here's how faith-based organizations can set themselves up for success:

- **Define Clear Goals** – Each piece of content should have a clear purpose: Is it for inspiration, education, engagement, or fundraising? Defining goals ensures content aligns with the ministry's overall mission.

- **Develop a Content Calendar** – Align media releases with major ministry events, holidays, and sermon series. This structured approach helps maintain consistency and relevancy.

- **Leverage AI and Automation** – Use tools like content scheduling software and AI-assisted scripting to streamline planning and reduce manual workload.

- **Gather Resources Efficiently** – Plan shoots and gather all necessary materials in advance. This includes securing locations, identifying necessary equipment, and ensuring talent availability.

2. Production: Maximizing Resources for Impact

Producing content sustainably requires making the most of available resources while maintaining quality:

- **Batch Production** – Record multiple episodes, sermons, or interviews in one session to save time and resources.

- **Repurpose Live Events** – Transform weekly sermons or church events into various content forms, such as YouTube videos, podcasts, and social media clips.

- **Use Mobile & Low-Cost Equipment** – High production quality is achievable without expensive gear. Modern smartphones, affordable microphones, and well-lit environments can yield professional results.

- **Create a Simple, Repeatable Setup** – Standardizing production setups saves time. Keep a checklist for setting up lights, cameras, and microphones to ensure consistency.

3. Post-Production & Repurposing: Extending the Lifespan of Your Content

The key to a sustainable content workflow is maximizing each piece of content by repurposing it for multiple platforms:

- **Automate Editing Tasks** – Use AI-powered editing tools to auto-caption, transcribe, and generate clips from longer videos.

- **Streamline Editing Workflows** – Create standard templates for intros, overlays, and transitions to ensure branding consistency while speeding up post-production.

- **Repurpose One Content Piece into Many** – Convert sermons into blog posts, infographics, short-form social media content, and even newsletters.

- **Optimize for Different Platforms** – Tailor content formats and lengths for various platforms (e.g., short clips for Instagram, long-form for YouTube, audio-only for podcasts).

Building a Team to Support Long-Term Success

Even with a solid workflow, having the right team in place is essential. Here's how to structure an effective media team:

- **Define Clear Roles** – Whether volunteers or professionals, ensure team members understand their responsibilities (content creation, editing, social media management, etc.).

- **Balance In-House and Outsourcing** – Determine which tasks can be handled internally and when to bring in external experts for specialized work.

- **Empower and Train Your Team** – Invest in skill-building through training sessions and mentorship to ensure your team stays current with media trends and technology.

Technology & Tools for Efficiency

To maintain sustainability, ministries should leverage technology to enhance efficiency:

- **Cloud-Based Collaboration** – Tools like Google Drive, Notion, and Asana help teams stay organized and track progress on content production.

- **Livestreaming Solutions** – Platforms like Restream, StreamYard, and Ecamm Live simplify livestreaming while maintaining high production quality.

- **AI-Powered Content Management** – Use AI tools for content scheduling, transcription, and social media automation to reduce workload.

Developing a Workflow that Aligns with Your Ministry's Mission

Each ministry has unique needs, so workflows must be adaptable while remaining structured. Consider these key steps:

1. **Assess Your Capacity** – Determine how much content your team can realistically produce without compromising quality.

2. **Create a Step-by-Step Production Guide** – Document processes so new team members can quickly integrate into the workflow.

3. **Schedule Regular Review Meetings** – Continuously optimize processes by assessing performance and making necessary adjustments.

4. **Build in Flexibility** – Leave room for spontaneous content while keeping a core workflow intact.

Setting the Stage for Audience Engagement

A well-structured production workflow is the foundation for deeper audience engagement. With an efficient system in place, ministries can focus on fostering two-way conversations, ensuring that content doesn't just reach audiences but also encourages meaningful interactions.

In the next chapter, we will explore how ministries can transform their media strategy from a one-way broadcast into an interactive community experience, deepening relationships with their audiences and strengthening engagement.

Lee Allen Miller

7 Engaging & Retaining Your Audience

Fostering Two-Way Conversations in Faith-Based Media

The Shift from One-Way to Two-Way Communication

For decades, faith-based media has primarily been a one-way street. Churches preached, radio stations broadcasted sermons, and television ministries aired carefully curated programs. Congregations and viewers listened. But they had limited opportunities to respond.

In today's media landscape, this model is rapidly becoming obsolete. Digital platforms have transformed communication into a two-way dialogue, where audiences expect interaction, engagement, and personal responses. Ministries that fail to embrace this shift risk losing their audience to more interactive and relational organizations.

Faith-based organizations that leverage two-way communication will not only maintain relevance but will cultivate deeper relationships, build stronger communities, and ultimately fulfill their mission more effectively. People no longer want to passively receive content—they want to participate in a shared spiritual journey.

This chapter will explore why fostering two-way conversations is essential for faith-based media, how to effectively implement interactive strategies, and how to overcome common challenges in audience engagement.

Why Two-Way Conversations Matter in Faith-Based Media

1. Trust and Community-Building

Trust is foundational in ministry. When audiences feel heard and valued, they develop a sense of belonging. Two-way conversations build relationships rather than just increasing viewership.

Ministries that engage with their followers personally—by responding to comments, addressing concerns, and celebrating milestones—become trusted spiritual guides rather than faceless content creators.

2. Authenticity Over Performance

Today's audience, particularly younger generations, crave authenticity. Highly produced content alone is not enough. They want real, meaningful interactions. Responding to their comments, answering their questions, and showing vulnerability fosters genuine connection.

3. Discipleship Happens Through Conversation

Jesus taught through engagement—He asked questions, He listened, and He responded to real concerns. Digital engagement is an opportunity for modern ministries to do the same.

Encouraging audience participation can lead to deeper discipleship, as individuals feel more personally involved in their faith journey.

4. Data-Driven Benefits

When ministries actively engage their audience, it triggers algorithms on platforms like Facebook, Instagram, and YouTube to increase visibility. More engagement leads to more reach, stronger relationships, and ultimately more support in the form of attendance, donations, and volunteerism.

The Channels for Two-Way Conversations

There are multiple platforms where ministries can create meaningful engagement. Understanding how to use each effectively is key to building a strong media presence.

1. Social Media Engagement

- **Responding to Comments & Messages:** A simple "thank you" or thoughtful response to a comment can make a huge impact.

- **Interactive Posts:** Use polls, Q&A sessions, and discussion prompts to invite audience participation.

- **User-Generated Content:** Encourage followers to share their testimonies, prayer requests, and faith experiences.

2. Live Streaming Interaction

- **Real-Time Q&A:** Engage with viewers during live sermons or discussions by answering their questions in real-time.

- **Dedicated Moderators:** Assign team members to engage in live chat conversations.

- **Interactive Features:** Utilize Facebook Stars, YouTube Super Chats, and Instagram Live Q&As to encourage participation.

3. Email and Messaging Platforms

- **Personalized Responses:** Use automation wisely but ensure genuine human interaction in responses.

- **Text-Based Ministry:** Offer prayer request text lines or devotionals via SMS to create intimate and accessible engagement.

4. Church Apps and Private Groups

- **Exclusive Communities:** Create private Facebook groups or app-based forums where members can discuss faith topics, prayer requests, and devotionals.

- **Moderated Discussions:** Ensure that conversations remain constructive and aligned with the ministry's mission.

5. AI and Automation Without Losing the Personal Touch

- **Chatbots for FAQs:** Use AI-powered chatbots for basic inquiries, but ensure human interaction for more complex discussions.

- **Scheduled Check-Ins:** Automate reminders, prayer requests, and event updates, but personalize responses when possible.

Engaging and Retaining the Audience

To keep people engaged, ministries need to go beyond creating content—they need to foster relationships. Here's how:

Encourage Participation

Instead of simply posting content, ask for feedback and discussion. Examples:

- "What is one way you have seen God move in your life this week?"

- "Share your favorite Bible verse and why it resonates with you."

Highlight Real Stories from the Community

Spotlight testimonials and faith journeys from your audience. People connect with real experiences more than abstract teachings.

Incentivize Deeper Engagement

- Offer exclusive content or behind-the-scenes access to those who actively engage.

- Run contests or challenges, such as "30 Days of Prayer" where participants share their reflections daily.

Addressing Challenges in Two-Way Conversations

1. Handling Criticism and Negative Comments

- Respond with grace and biblical wisdom rather than defensiveness.

- If a comment thread becomes hostile, direct the conversation to private messages or a phone call.

- Know when to engage and when to ignore; not every comment deserves a response.

2. Avoiding Over-Reliance on Automation

While tools like chatbots and automated responses can be helpful, they should not replace genuine human interaction. Personal engagement should always be prioritized.

3. Maintaining Theological Integrity

Open discussions are great, but they should align with sound biblical teaching. Ministries should set clear guidelines on respectful and doctrinally sound discussions.

Practical Steps to Foster Two-Way Engagement

1. Establish a Digital Engagement Team

Have dedicated team members responsible for monitoring comments, responding to messages, and fostering discussions.

2. Train Leaders to Be Conversational

Pastors and media personalities should be approachable and willing to engage, not just preach.

3. Set Clear Engagement Goals

Define what meaningful engagement looks like for your ministry:

- Increasing social media interaction by 30%.

- Responding to 100% of prayer requests within 24 hours.

- Hosting at least one interactive live session per month.

4. Utilize Analytics to Refine Engagement Strategies

- Track comment and message response rates.

- Assess engagement trends and adjust content accordingly.

Moving from Viewers to Disciples

Two-way conversations are the future of faith-based media. Ministries that embrace interactive engagement will foster deeper discipleship, build stronger communities, and enhance their mission's impact. The goal is no longer just to broadcast messages—it's to create spaces where believers can connect, grow, and thrive together.

By fostering genuine conversations, ministries move beyond simply reaching people to **truly engaging** them, strengthening their faith journey in the digital era.

Leveraging Analytics to Optimize Your Strategy: The Power of Data in Faith-Based Media

In today's media landscape, analytics is no longer optional—it's essential. Ministries and faith-based organizations must understand their audience's behaviors, preferences, and engagement patterns to maximize their impact. Analytics provides invaluable insights that help refine messaging, optimize outreach strategies, and ensure resources are being used effectively. But data should not replace faith-driven decision-making; rather, it should serve as a guide to enhance and inform ministry strategies.

Key Metrics to Track Across Media Platforms

Social Media Analytics

- **Engagement Rate:** Measures interactions (likes, shares, comments) to assess content effectiveness.

- **Reach & Impressions:** Helps determine how far your message is spreading.

- **Follower Growth:** Indicates audience expansion and long-term reach.

- **Content Performance:** Identifies which posts resonate most with your audience.

Streaming & Video Analytics

- **Watch Time & Retention Rates:** Shows how much of a video is being watched before viewers drop off.

- **Click-Through Rate (CTR):** Measures how effective your titles and thumbnails are in attracting viewers.

- **Live vs. On-Demand Engagement:** Helps determine the best format for delivering messages.

Broadcast & Cable Analytics

- **Viewership Trends:** Understanding peak times and demographic insights.

- **Call-to-Action Response Rates:** Measures the effectiveness of on-air appeals for donations or engagement.

Fundraising & Digital Giving Analytics

- **Donation Trends:** Tracks giving habits to identify donor retention opportunities.

- **Recurring Donors vs. One-Time Givers:** Helps shape fundraising strategies for long-term sustainability.

- **Conversion Rates on Giving Pages:** Identifies how well donation pages are performing.

How to Use Data to Strengthen Your Media Strategy

Refining Messaging Based on Audience Insights

Analyzing which messages drive the most engagement allows ministries to tailor content that resonates deeply with their audience. A church noticing that short-form inspirational clips outperform hour-long sermons might pivot to more bite-sized content formats.

Optimizing Content Schedules Based on Peak Engagement

Understanding when your audience is most active can enhance outreach effectiveness. If analytics show that Facebook engagement peaks on Wednesday evenings, scheduling posts at that time increases visibility and interaction.

Data-Driven Decision Making for Better Resource Allocation

Analytics can reveal which platforms and content types generate the most impact, helping ministries allocate budgets and personnel efficiently. If a digital campaign drives more conversions than a traditional mail campaign, shifting resources accordingly can maximize reach and engagement.

Balancing Data & Spirit-Led Decision Making

The Risk of Over-Reliance on Analytics

While data provides critical insights, faith-based media leaders must ensure that numerical trends do not override spiritual discernment. Not all successful content metrics equate to impactful ministry outcomes.

Using Analytics as a Tool, Not a Crutch

Data should serve as a guiding mechanism rather than a decision-making substitute. Just because one type of content performs well in numbers doesn't mean it's always the most spiritually nourishing option.

Faith-Driven Data Interpretation

Analytics should be assessed through the lens of mission alignment. A campaign that generates thousands of views but lacks engagement or action may need re-evaluation.

Practical Steps for Ministries to Implement Analytics

1. **Use the Right Tools:** Leverage platforms like Google Analytics, Facebook Insights, YouTube Studio, and email marketing reports.

2. **Establish an Analytics Review Process:** Schedule regular reviews of key performance indicators (KPIs) to adjust strategies as needed.

3. **Translate Insights into Action:** Ensure data leads to concrete changes, such as refining sermon delivery formats or adjusting social media posting schedules.

Case Studies of Successful Data-Driven Ministries

Case Study 1: A Church Growing Through Digital Analytics

A mid-sized church struggling with declining in-person attendance leveraged Facebook and YouTube analytics to refine their digital strategy. By tracking peak engagement times and sermon drop-off points, they adapted their content into shorter, high-impact sermon snippets, leading to increased digital attendance and eventual physical service growth.

Case Study 2: A Faith-Based Nonprofit Increasing Donations

A faith-based nonprofit noticed a plateau in donations. Through analytics, they discovered that donors engaged more with video storytelling over static fundraising emails. They pivoted to producing donor-impact videos, leading to a 40% increase in recurring donations.

Engagement Elements & Reader Takeaways

Quick Wins

- Start by tracking engagement rates on one primary platform before expanding to others.

- A/B test different content styles to see what resonates most with your audience.

Pro Tips

- Set up Google Analytics goals to track conversions on donation pages.

- Use social media insights to determine the best times for engagement-driven posts.

Reflection Questions

1. What analytics do you currently track, and how do they inform your strategy?

2. Are there areas where you might be over-relying on data instead of faith-driven decision-making?

3. How can you use analytics to better serve and engage your audience?

Leveraging analytics effectively requires a balance of **data-driven insights and spiritual discernment**. Ministries that harness these tools wisely can optimize their outreach, deepen audience engagement, and ensure every piece of content is aligned with their mission. With the right approach, analytics transforms from mere numbers into a **powerful instrument for meaningful, faith-centered impact.**

From Viewers to Active Participants: Strengthening Community Engagement

The Shift from Audience to Community

In today's media-driven world, ministries and faith-based organizations have unprecedented access to audiences. Whether through social media, streaming platforms, or broadcast networks, reaching people has never been easier. However, with this expanded reach comes a new challenge: how to turn passive viewers into engaged, committed participants in your ministry. Viewership alone is no longer enough; true Impact happens when an audience becomes a thriving, interactive community.

A faith-based media strategy should not just focus on content distribution but on fostering meaningful connections that inspire action. The goal is to move beyond passive consumption and cultivate a sense of belonging—transforming viewers into active contributors to the mission.

The Engagement Funnel: Turning Viewers into Participants

To effectively transition viewers into active community members, ministries must understand the engagement funnel, a structured pathway that moves audiences from casual observers to fully invested participants.

1. **Awareness:** Viewers discover your content through social media, television, radio, or live streams.

2. **Interaction:** Audiences begin liking, commenting, and sharing content, showing initial engagement.

3. **Commitment:** Viewers take further steps, such as joining a mailing list, following a Bible study plan, or attending live events.

4. **Community:** Individuals become actively involved by volunteering, donating, or leading local and online faith groups.

Each stage requires intentional strategies to help people take the next step from passive engagement to active involvement.

Practical Strategies for Engagement

1. Interactive Content That Inspires Engagement

Modern audiences expect interaction, not just one-way communication. Ministries must integrate **real-time engagement** opportunities into their content:

- **Live Q&A Sessions:** Host live discussions where pastors and ministry leaders answer audience questions in real time.

- **Interactive Polls & Surveys:** Use Instagram Stories, Facebook Polls, or Twitter Q&A to invite audience input on faith-based topics.

- **Call-In Shows:** Encourage radio and television audiences to call in and share their testimonies or ask theological questions.

- **Live Chat on Streams:** Train digital hosts to welcome viewers, answer comments, and facilitate discussions during live broadcasts.

2. Creating Community-Building Spaces

True engagement happens when people feel they belong. Ministries can foster this sense of belonging by building **community-focused digital spaces**:

- **Facebook & WhatsApp Groups:** Create small digital fellowship groups where members can discuss sermons, share prayer requests, and offer support.

- **Private Membership Platforms:** Use tools like Mighty Networks or a custom church app to provide exclusive Bible studies, live sessions, and community discussions.

- **Virtual Bible Studies & Prayer Groups:** Host weekly online meetings where viewers can connect, discuss scripture, and grow in faith together.

3. Encouraging User-Generated Content

People engage most when they feel their voices are heard. Ministries should empower their community members to share their own faith journeys:

- **Testimonies & Storytelling:** Feature user-submitted stories about how faith has impacted their lives.

- **Hashtag Campaigns:** Create a unique hashtag (e.g., #FaithInAction) and encourage people to share their spiritual experiences.

- **Creative Contributions:** Invite members to submit devotional reflections, artwork, music, or spoken word pieces that can be featured in ministry content.

4. Consistent Call to Action (CTA)

A clear and compelling CTA encourages viewers to take action. Every piece of content—whether a sermon, social post, or broadcast—should include a specific invitation:

- "Join our weekly online Bible study."

- "Share your testimony with us."

- "Comment below with your favorite scripture."

- "Sign up to serve in your community."

CTAs should be simple, actionable, and directly tied to deepening engagement.

Leveraging Technology to Drive Engagement

1. AI-Powered Personalization

Artificial Intelligence (AI) can help ministries recommend personalized faith-based content to viewers, increasing engagement:

- **Automated Chatbots:** AI chatbots on ministry websites can answer FAQs, recommend sermons, and pray for users.

- **Smart Content Recommendations:** Platforms like YouTube and Facebook suggest personalized sermon clips based on previous engagement.

2. Web3 & Decentralized Communities

Blockchain and Web3 technologies offer new opportunities for faith-based engagement:

- **NFT-Based Memberships:** Exclusive digital collectibles that unlock special content or community access.

- **Decentralized Giving Platforms:** Secure, transparent donation systems using blockchain.

3. Virtual Reality (VR) & Augmented Reality (AR)

Emerging technology can enhance spiritual experiences:

- **VR Worship Services:** Virtual reality church services allow members from around the world to worship together in immersive environments.

- **Augmented Reality Bible Studies:** AR apps bring scripture to life, offering interactive experiences for deeper study.

Case Studies: Ministries That Transformed Viewers into Engaged Communities

1. Elevation Church: Digital Discipleship

Elevation Church has successfully built an online ecosystem where viewers progress from watching sermons to engaging in community groups and leadership training. Their **eGroups (online small groups)** foster deep, sustained engagement beyond Sunday services.

2. The Chosen: Interactive Storytelling

This faith-based streaming series actively involves its audience through interactive social campaigns, crowdfunding initiatives, and behind-the-scenes engagement. Fans feel like **co-creators**, increasing loyalty and community strength.

3. YouVersion Bible App: Personalized Engagement

YouVersion turned passive Bible reading into an interactive experience with daily devotionals, scripture challenges, and social sharing features, making scripture engagement a **community-driven** experience.

Measuring Success: Key Metrics for Engagement

To understand how well a ministry is converting viewers into active participants, track these engagement metrics:

- **Comment & Interaction Rate:** The number of comments, replies, and shares on social media.

- **Participation in Groups:** Growth and activity in online communities.

- **Volunteer Sign-Ups:** Number of viewers moving into action through service and ministry involvement.

- **User-Generated Content Contributions:** How often viewers submit testimonies, artwork, or devotional reflections.

The Long-Term Vision: Sustainable Community Growth

Strengthening community engagement is not a one-time initiative but a long-term commitment. Ministries should:

- **Develop Digital Discipleship Pathways:** Guide viewers through structured next steps in their faith journey.

- **Train Digital Ambassadors:** Equip volunteers to serve as online community leaders.

- **Emphasize Two-Way Communication:** Make engagement a conversation, not just a broadcast.

Engaged Communities Create Lasting Impact

Transitioning from passive viewership to active participation is the key to lasting ministry impact. By integrating interactive content, leveraging technology, and fostering true community, ministries can build deep, meaningful relationships that go beyond a single broadcast or social media post. When people move from being consumers of faith-based content to engaged contributors in their faith community, the mission of spreading the Gospel takes on an unstoppable momentum.

Lee Allen Miller

8 Fundraising & Monetization in the Digital Age

Digital Giving - Engaging Modern Donors: The Shift Toward Digital Giving in Ministry

In the past, tithes and offerings were collected exclusively in person—passed in offering plates, received in church envelopes, or even dropped in donation boxes. But today's donors live in a digital-first world. They expect **convenience, security, and multiple options** when it comes to giving. If ministries fail to offer these, they risk losing valuable financial support.

Digital giving isn't just a convenience—it's the **lifeline of modern ministries**. Nonprofits, churches, and faith-based organizations that embrace digital giving see increased engagement, more predictable donations, and greater financial stability. Studies show that organizations using digital-first fundraising strategies experience **higher donor retention rates** and larger overall contributions.

The church is not immune to these changes. Faith-based organizations that continue relying solely on **traditional tithing models** risk falling behind. Digital giving is no longer a backup option—it's a primary **vehicle for sustaining ministry impact**.

Key Insight: The shift to digital is not about replacing faith-based generosity—it's about facilitating it.

Understanding the Modern Donor Mindset

To engage today's donors, ministries must understand what drives them to give. The modern donor is **mobile-first, values impact, and expects transparency**.

- **Younger generations (Millennials & Gen Z) are digital natives.** They are less likely to carry cash or write checks but are **more likely to set up recurring donations**.

- **Trust and transparency matter.** Donors want to see where their money goes and how it makes an impact. Ministries that communicate **clear, measurable results** build stronger donor relationships.

- **Ease of giving is critical.** If donating takes too many steps, potential donors abandon the process. The fewer clicks, the better.

Pro Tip: Ministries that use storytelling to highlight the impact of donations see **higher giving rates**. Show the mission in action.

Best Practices for Implementing Digital Giving

Choosing the Right Digital Giving Platform

There are **hundreds** of online giving tools available. The best platforms for faith-based organizations include:

- **Tithe.ly** - Designed for churches with text, app, and online giving options.

- **Pushpay** - A seamless giving experience with automation and donor management.

- **PayPal for Nonprofits** - Widely trusted and easy to integrate into any website.

When selecting a platform, consider **fees, recurring donation capabilities, and ease of integration** with your ministry's website.

Offering Multiple Ways to Give

A one-size-fits-all approach won't work. Ministries need to provide **various donation options** to meet people where they are:

- **Website Giving** – A simple, well-placed "Donate" button on your homepage.

- **Text-to-Give** – Allows donors to send donations via text message instantly.

- **QR Codes** – Scannable codes placed in bulletins, screens, and event banners.

- **App-Based Giving** – Integrated into ministry apps, making giving easier on mobile.

- **Social Media Giving** – Facebook Fundraisers, Instagram donation stickers, and YouTube's donate button.

Pro Tip: Churches that offer **recurring giving options** see more consistent and reliable financial support.

Leveraging Social Media & Streaming for Fundraising

Live Appeal Giving

Encourage donations in **real-time** during live streams and church services by:

- Displaying a **giving link or QR code** during the broadcast.

- Using a **giving thermometer** to show progress in fundraising campaigns.

- Offering **matching challenges** to encourage more participation.

Social Media Fundraising Campaigns

Social media isn't just for outreach—it's for fundraising, too. Ways to drive digital giving include:

- **Facebook Fundraisers** – Allow church members to create personal campaigns.

- **Instagram Stories Donations** – Using stickers to encourage small, one-time gifts.

- **Hashtag Challenges** – Engage the community by linking giving to online participation.

Case Study: A church launched a **24-hour giving challenge** on Facebook with a donor match campaign. By the end of the day, they raised 3x their typical weekly giving.

Transparency & Accountability in Digital Giving

Trust is the foundation of generosity. Donors want to know how their contributions are used. Ministries that provide clear financial reporting and impact stories build lasting trust.

Best Practices for Donor Retention

1. **Regular updates** – Share progress reports on how donations are making an impact.

132

2. **Thank-you messages** – A personalized thank-you email or video fosters connection.

3. **Exclusive donor content** – Provide behind-the-scenes access or special updates.

Avoiding Common Pitfalls

- **Stay compliant** – Ensure tax-exempt status and proper donation tracking.

- **Protect donor data** – Use **secure payment processors** to prevent fraud.

- **Avoid pushy requests** – Engage donors with **mission-driven messaging**, not guilt.

Case Study: A Ministry That Mastered Digital Giving

A mid-sized church in Texas saw **a 45% increase in total giving** after implementing a multi-platform digital strategy. Key success factors:

- **Launched a text-to-give campaign** with clear instructions in every service.

- **Implemented recurring giving** options with monthly "impact reports."

- **Used Facebook Live donation appeals** during community service events.

- **Created video testimonies** showing how digital donations changed lives.

The Future of Faith-Based Fundraising

The next generation of digital giving includes:

- **AI-driven donor engagement** – Personalized giving suggestions based on donor history.

- **Blockchain transparency** – Donors see exactly where their money goes.

- **Cryptocurrency and NFT fundraising** – Exploring new ways to engage tech-savvy givers.

Key Insight: Faith-based organizations that stay **ahead of digital trends** will be best positioned to sustain long-term impact.

A Call to Action

Digital giving is more than a **transaction**—it's an **opportunity for engagement** and **sustainable ministry growth**. Ministries that embrace digital giving create **a culture of generosity** that fuels long-term impact.

Challenge: What digital giving method will you implement this week? Start small, build consistency, and trust God to provide.

Final Thought: **When giving is easy, generosity thrives.**

Subscription Models, Crowdfunding, and Other Revenue Streams

Introduction

Faith-based media has entered a new era of digital engagement, where ministries and faith-driven organizations must think beyond traditional donations and tithing to sustain their mission. While contributions from dedicated supporters remain foundational, the rise of subscription models, crowdfunding, and alternative revenue streams presents new opportunities for financial sustainability.

To thrive in this changing landscape, faith-based leaders must embrace innovative funding models that align with their values while also engaging their audience in meaningful ways. This chapter explores how ministries can implement subscription-based content, leverage crowdfunding, and tap into diverse revenue streams while remaining mission-focused.

The Subscription Economy in Faith-Based Media

The Shift Toward Membership Models

The subscription economy has reshaped consumer expectations. Platforms like Netflix, Disney+, and Spotify have conditioned audiences to access premium content through recurring memberships. Faith-based media can leverage this model to create sustainable revenue while offering exclusive, high-value content to supporters.

How Ministries Can Implement a Subscription Model

Ministries and Christian content creators can structure subscription offerings in several ways:

- **Tiered Memberships:** Offering different levels of access, such as exclusive Bible studies, behind-the-scenes content, or early access to sermons.

- **Premium Video Content:** Faith-based streaming services like PureFlix have demonstrated the viability of subscription-based Christian entertainment.

- **Community-Based Subscriptions:** Providing access to a private prayer group, faith-driven discussion forums, or mentorship programs.

- **Bonus Digital Resources:** Monthly devotionals, e-books, or exclusive faith-based courses.

Balancing Accessibility and Revenue

While monetization is necessary, ministries must balance paid content with free resources. A successful model blends premium experiences with freely available faith-based teachings, ensuring financial support doesn't become a barrier to spiritual engagement.

Crowdfunding as a Community-Driven Funding Model

The Power of Collective Giving

Crowdfunding harnesses the power of a community to fund specific projects, initiatives, or ongoing ministry efforts. Rather than relying on a few major donors, this model encourages widespread participation, allowing many individuals to contribute in small amounts toward a shared mission.

Keys to a Successful Crowdfunding Campaign

1. **Clear Vision:** Define a compelling purpose for your campaign—whether it's launching a new podcast, funding a church plant, or expanding a digital ministry.

2. **Storytelling Matters:** Share personal testimonies, impact stories, and the mission behind the campaign.

3. **Incentives and Rewards:** Offer tiered giving incentives, such as early access to content, personalized thank-you messages, or limited-edition faith-based merchandise.

4. **Regular Updates and Transparency:** Keep supporters engaged with campaign progress, testimonials, and financial transparency.

5. **Choose the Right Platform:** Utilize crowdfunding sites such as GoFundMe, Kickstarter, or faith-specific platforms like GiveSendGo.

Case Study: How Ministries Have Successfully Used Crowdfunding

Many ministries and faith-driven content creators have successfully funded projects through crowdfunding. For example, a Christian media organization launched a documentary series on biblical history through Kickstarter, surpassing their goal due to strong community engagement. By sharing a clear vision, engaging their audience, and maintaining transparency, they cultivated a community of financial supporters.

Alternative Revenue Streams for Faith-Based Media

1. Sponsorships & Strategic Partnerships

Brands and organizations that align with Christian values can serve as sponsors for digital events, podcasts, or online courses. Sponsored content, when chosen carefully, can enhance ministry efforts without compromising integrity.

Examples:

- Faith-based book publishers sponsoring a ministry's podcast.

- Christian businesses underwriting the cost of an online conference.

2. Affiliate Marketing & Merchandise Sales

Faith-based organizations can generate income through affiliate marketing and branded merchandise.

- **Affiliate Marketing:** Promoting Christian books, apps, or faith-based services with commission-based referral links.

- **Branded Merchandise:** Selling T-shirts, mugs, journals, or artwork featuring scripture-based messages, reinforcing ministry branding while generating revenue.

3. Live Events & Conferences

Monetizing faith-based conferences, summits, or online workshops provides another revenue opportunity. Ticketed events with a combination of free and premium access levels encourage wider participation while sustaining the organization financially.

4. Licensing and Content Syndication

Faith-based media organizations can license their content to other networks, streaming platforms, or radio stations. For instance, a ministry producing high-quality sermon videos can license them to Christian TV networks, creating an additional revenue stream.

Best Practices for Long-Term Financial Sustainability

1. **Maintain Financial Integrity:** Ensure transparency in how funds are used and regularly communicate financial impact to supporters.

2. **Diversify Revenue Streams:** Avoid relying too heavily on a single income source. A balanced mix of subscriptions, crowdfunding, sponsorships, and merchandise sales enhances stability.

3. **Engage Your Audience Consistently:** Strong donor relationships stem from ongoing engagement, updates, and personalized appreciation for contributions.

4. **Align Revenue with Mission:** Any revenue-generating effort should reflect the core mission and values of the faith-based organization.

5. **Leverage Technology Wisely:** Use digital tools for seamless subscription management, donation tracking, and engagement analytics.

Embracing Innovation While Staying Mission-Focused

The digital landscape presents abundant opportunities for faith-based media to thrive. By integrating subscription models, crowdfunding, and alternative revenue streams, ministries can achieve financial sustainability without compromising their core mission.

As you explore these strategies, remain prayerful, adaptable, and mission-driven. Whether through memberships, community-funded projects, or digital products, the ultimate goal is to serve

God's kingdom effectively while ensuring your media ministry remains financially resilient.

The world is changing, and faith-based media must evolve with it. The question is not *whether* to innovate—it's *how* to do so while staying true to the message. Now is the time to embrace new models of sustainability, ensuring that faith-driven content reaches and impacts audiences for generations to come.

Leveraging Web3 & Blockchain for Faith-Based Fundraising

Introduction: A New Era of Giving

The digital age has transformed the way ministries and faith-based organizations reach, engage, and serve their communities. While traditional fundraising methods like tithes, offerings, and capital campaigns continue to be essential, the rise of **Web3 and blockchain** presents a groundbreaking opportunity to enhance **transparency, security, and donor engagement**.

For faith-based organizations, adopting blockchain technology isn't about following a trend; it's about leveraging **new tools that align with biblical principles of stewardship, accountability, and generosity**. This chapter explores how ministries can integrate **cryptocurrency donations, smart contracts, NFTs, and decentralized finance (DeFi)** to create a more engaging and effective fundraising model.

The Case for Blockchain in Faith-Based Giving

Blockchain technology is revolutionizing financial transactions by providing a **decentralized, transparent, and immutable ledger**. For faith-based fundraising, this means:

1. Increased Trust and Transparency

- Every donation is recorded on a **public ledger**, allowing complete visibility into how funds are used.

- Donors can **track their impact** in real time, fostering trust and deeper engagement.

- Eliminates concerns over mismanagement or lack of financial clarity.

2. Lower Transaction Fees, More Direct Impact

- Traditional donation platforms take anywhere from **2% to 10%** in processing fees.

- **Cryptocurrency transactions** often have lower fees, ensuring more funds go directly to ministry initiatives.

- **Smart contracts** automate fund distribution, eliminating unnecessary middlemen.

3. Borderless Giving: Global Donations with No Restrictions

- Enables **cross-border giving** without worrying about currency exchange rates or international fees.

- Supports **missionary work, disaster relief, and church planting** in countries with limited banking access.

Faith-Based Use Cases for Blockchain in Fundraising

The opportunities for faith-based organizations to leverage Web3 are vast. Below are some **real-world applications** ministries can implement today.

1. Accepting Cryptocurrency Donations

Many churches and ministries are now accepting **Bitcoin (BTC), Ethereum (ETH), and stablecoins** as donations.

Steps to Get Started:

1. **Set up a Crypto Wallet** – Use platforms like **Engiven, The Giving Block, or Coinbase Commerce**.

2. **Educate Your Congregation** – Provide resources on the benefits and process of crypto giving.

3. **Integrate with Church Websites & Apps** – Allow for seamless online transactions.

4. **Ensure Compliance** – Work with tax professionals to manage cryptocurrency reporting.

2. Smart Contracts for Automated Giving

A **smart contract** is a blockchain-based contract that **automatically executes transactions when conditions are met**.

How Ministries Can Use Smart Contracts:

- **Tithing Automation:** Members can set up smart contracts to **automatically send their tithe** on payday.

- **Mission Fund Disbursement:** Donations for specific projects (church building, disaster relief, etc.) can be **automatically distributed** to the right accounts.

- **Endowments & Trusts:** Long-term funds can be **securely allocated and released** according to predefined conditions.

3. NFTs (Non-Fungible Tokens) for Digital Engagement

NFTs provide a unique way to **fundraise while offering value in return**.

Creative NFT Applications for Ministries:

- **Commemorative Digital Art:** Soll NFT baood ecripturo art, digital crosses, or special event memorabilia.

- **Exclusive Access Passes:** Provide donors with NFTs that grant access to **exclusive sermons, courses, or live Q&A sessions**.

- **Mission Impact Badges:** Donors receive an NFT recognizing their contribution, creating a **digital legacy of giving**.

4. Tokenized Impact Projects

Blockchain allows ministries to **tokenize impact projects**, meaning that every donation is linked to a **real, trackable outcome**.

Examples:

- A church fundraising for a new **water well in Africa** can issue digital tokens that show **when the well is funded, built, and operational**.

- A disaster relief organization can provido **real-timc tracking** of how funds are being allocated and spent.

Implementing Web3 in Your Organization

Adopting Web3 for faith-based fundraising requires careful planning. Here's a step-by-step approach to integrating these technologies:

Step 1: Build Awareness & Education

- Educate your leadership team and congregation on **blockchain, crypto, and Web3**.

- Host **informational sessions** or partner with experts to provide guidance.

- Address **common misconceptions** about blockchain and its ethical use in faith-based organizations.

Step 2: Establish Secure Donation Infrastructure

- Set up a **secure crypto wallet** (e.g., **MetaMask, Trust Wallet, Coinbase Commerce**).

- Work with **Web3-enabled donation platforms** like **Engiven or The Giving Block**.

- Integrate crypto donation buttons on your **website, mobile app, and social media**.

Step 3: Legal & Financial Compliance

- Ensure your organization complies with **tax regulations** on crypto donations.

- Provide **tax receipts for donors** using crypto.

- Work with financial advisors to manage blockchain-based assets responsibly.

Step 4: Launch & Promote Web3 Giving Options

- Create a **marketing campaign** to introduce your faith community to Web3 giving.

- Showcase **success stories** from other churches and ministries using blockchain.

- Encourage early adopters to **share their experiences**.

Overcoming Challenges & Ethical Considerations

While blockchain offers **exciting opportunities**, ministries must also navigate challenges carefully.

1. Addressing Volatility Concerns

- Use **stablecoins (e.g., USDC, DAI) to avoid market fluctuations**.

- Convert cryptocurrency donations to fiat immediately to **minimize risk**.

2. Ensuring Alignment with Faith-Based Values

- Some view cryptocurrency as speculative or risky—**education is key**.

- Emphasize **stewardship and responsible use** of funds.

- Choose projects that promote **honesty, transparency, and social good**.

3. Regulatory & Tax Implications

- Stay updated on **government policies regarding crypto donations**.

- Partner with **legal and financial experts** to ensure compliance.

- Provide **clear tax reporting** for donors and your organization.

The Future of Web3 & Faith-Based Fundraising

The adoption of Web3 technologies in faith-based giving is still in its early stages, but the potential is **immense**.

Emerging Trends to Watch:

- **Faith-Based DAOs (Decentralized Autonomous Organizations):** Community-driven funding models for missions.

- **Metaverse Churches:** Virtual faith communities built in digital spaces.

- **Blockchain-Based Humanitarian Aid:** Transparent and trackable distribution of relief funds.

Faith-based organizations that embrace these technologies today will **not only reach younger, tech-savvy donors** but will also create **sustainable, transparent, and innovative fundraising models** that stand the test of time.

Stepping into the Future with Faith

Integrating **Web3 and blockchain** into faith-based fundraising is not just about keeping up with technology—it's about **enhancing stewardship, trust, and impact** in ways never before possible. By **embracing innovation while staying rooted in biblical**

principles, ministries can **unlock new opportunities for generosity and outreach**. The future of faith-based giving is decentralized, transparent, and full of possibility. Now is the time to take the first step.

Lee Allen Miller

9 Overcoming Common Challenges in Media Integration

Bridging the Gap Between Digital & Traditional Teams: The Growing Divide in Faith-Based Media

Faith-based media organizations are facing a significant challenge—an internal divide between traditional media teams and digital-first content creators. The rapid evolution of digital platforms has forced organizations to rethink their outreach strategies, but many ministries and broadcasters are struggling to integrate these two worlds effectively.

Traditional media teams—those specializing in television, radio, and print—have long mastered high-quality, professionally produced content. They are accustomed to structured programming schedules, formal distribution channels, and established viewership habits. Meanwhile, digital teams thrive on agility, rapid content production, and real-time audience engagement across social media, streaming platforms, and emerging technologies.

When these teams fail to work together, the result is a disjointed media strategy that confuses audiences, weakens outreach efforts, and creates inefficiencies. Ministries risk losing impact if their content lacks consistency across platforms, and audiences accustomed to seamless digital experiences may disengage from organizations that appear fragmented.

The good news? The gap between traditional and digital teams is not insurmountable. With the right strategies, faith-based media organizations can foster collaboration, build unified workflows, and maximize the strengths of both worlds to create a powerhouse media presence.

Why Bridging the Gap is Essential

A unified media strategy is critical for faith-based organizations aiming to expand their reach. Ministries can no longer afford to treat digital and traditional media as separate entities. To be effective, they must integrate these teams to achieve:

- **Consistent Messaging:** Faith-based media must ensure that the messages shared on TV, radio, and print align seamlessly with social media, websites, and streaming platforms.

- **Expanded Audience Reach:** Traditional media still holds influence, but digital platforms allow organizations to engage with younger, tech-savvy audiences in real-time.

- **Efficiency & Cost Savings:** Rather than duplicating efforts, integrated teams can repurpose content, streamline workflows, and optimize production resources.

- **Better Engagement & Community Building:** Digital media fosters two-way conversations, allowing ministries to build deeper relationships with their audience.

Steps to Bridging the Gap

1. Shift the Mindset: From Silos to Synergy

A key barrier to integration is the mindset difference between teams. Traditional media professionals often view digital as less polished or lacking credibility, while digital teams may see traditional approaches as outdated and slow-moving. The solution lies in fostering mutual respect and emphasizing that both methods serve a crucial purpose.

Action Steps:

- **Leadership Buy-In:** Leaders must champion integration by clearly articulating the vision for a unified media strategy.

- **Team Discussions:** Facilitate regular meetings where digital and traditional teams share insights, challenges, and success stories.

- **Cross-Training:** Encourage team members to learn from one another—traditional teams can gain digital skills, while digital teams can adopt professional storytolling techniques.

2. Invest in Training & Upskilling

Many traditional media professionals are not resistant to digital but lack the skills to navigate the fast-paced world of social media, streaming, and online engagement. Conversely, digital creators may need training in structured content production and broadcast-quality storytelling.

Action Steps:

- Provide training sessions on digital trends, analytics, and content repurposing for traditional teams.

- Offer storytelling workshops for digital teams to improve content quality and alignment with long-form programming.

- Encourage collaboration on projects to create hybrid content that blends traditional depth with digital engagement.

3. Create Cross-Team Collaboration Workflows

One of the biggest barriers to integration is a lack of structured collaboration. Digital and traditional teams often operate with different deadlines, tools, and expectations. By establishing clear workflows, organizations can facilitate seamless cooperation.

Action Steps:

- Use **project management tools** like Trello, Asana, or Monday.com to track content production and ensure alignment.

- Implement a **shared editorial calendar** to synchronize programming schedules with digital content rollouts.

- Assign **cross-functional teams** to major initiatives, ensuring that traditional and digital perspectives are incorporated from the start.

4. Leverage Technology & Automation

Technology can be a bridge that connects traditional and digital media efforts. Ministries can use automation and content management systems to ensure that one piece of content seamlessly flows across multiple platforms.

Action Steps:

- Use AI-driven transcription services to convert sermons and broadcasts into blog posts, social media snippets, and YouTube content.

- Implement scheduling tools to ensure social media promotions align with television and radio broadcasts.

- Integrate CRM systems to track audience engagement across both traditional and digital touchpoints.

5. Develop a Unified Content Strategy

A well-integrated media organization must operate from a single, cohesive content strategy. This means aligning messaging, visuals, and campaign themes across all platforms to create a consistent brand experience.

Action Steps:

- Establish clear content pillars that guide messaging across all media formats.

- Develop templates for repurposing traditional content into digital-friendly formats (e.g., turning a 30-minute sermon into short-form video clips, social media posts, and blog excerpts).

- Maintain a central repository where both teams can access branding guidelines, key messaging, and media assets.

Building a Culture of Innovation & Adaptation

The media landscape is constantly evolving, and organizations that refuse to adapt will struggle to maintain relevance. A key step in bridging the gap is fostering a culture of innovation where both traditional and digital teams are encouraged to experiment, test new approaches, and embrace continuous learning.

Action Steps:

- Organize monthly brainstorming sessions where both teams can pitch ideas for content, campaigns, and platform expansion.

- Celebrate successful collaborations to reinforce the value of integration.

- Provide team members with the freedom to test new digital strategies without fear of failure.

Looking Ahead: Preparing for Platform Changes & Algorithm Shifts

Bridging the gap between digital and traditional teams isn't just about solving today's challenges—it's about preparing for the future. The next chapter will explore how ministries and broadcasters can stay ahead of constant platform changes, algorithm shifts, and emerging trends that impact audience engagement. With a unified media team, faith-based organizations will be equipped to navigate the evolving digital landscape with agility and confidence.

By fostering collaboration, integrating workflows, and embracing new media approaches, ministries can build a powerhouse outreach strategy that stands the test of time. The future of faith-based media isn't an either/or proposition between digital and traditional—it's the seamless unification of both.

Navigating Platform Changes & Algorithm Shifts

Introduction: The Constant Evolution of Digital Media

The digital media landscape is constantly shifting, and for faith-based organizations, staying ahead isn't just a technical necessity—it's a strategic imperative. Social media algorithms, streaming policies, and broadcast regulations evolve rapidly, often leaving ministries scrambling to keep up. But the organizations that thrive aren't just reactive; they anticipate change and adapt proactively.

In this chapter, we'll break down the key shifts occurring across major digital platforms, discuss their impact on faith-based outreach, and explore strategies for adapting without losing authenticity or effectiveness. By the end, you'll have a roadmap for navigating the ever-changing digital landscape with confidence.

1. Understanding Algorithmic Changes: Why They Matter

Every platform—from Facebook to YouTube, TikTok to Instagram—relies on algorithms to determine what content gets seen and by whom. These changes are often motivated by shifts in user behavior, business models, and regulatory demands. Here's why staying informed about them is critical:

- **Visibility & Engagement:** Changes can drastically alter how many people see your content. A tweak in Facebook's feed algorithm, for example, could mean the difference between reaching thousands of followers organically or disappearing from their feeds entirely.

- **Content Prioritization:** Platforms often push new features (like Instagram Reels or YouTube Shorts) and reward users who adopt them early.

- **Compliance & Monetization:** Shifts in platform policies (such as YouTube's new rules for faith-based or sensitive content) can affect how ministries fundraise or distribute content.

Key Shift in 2024: Major platforms have deprioritized static posts in favor of **short-form video, AI-generated recommendations, and interactive content** (polls, live Q&A). Ministries that fail to embrace these trends risk a sharp decline in engagement.

Action Step: Regularly check platform blogs (Meta, YouTube Creator Insider, TikTok's newsroom) and follow trusted digital ministry consultants to stay ahead of updates.

2. Adapting Without Losing Your Message

One of the biggest challenges faith-based organizations face when algorithms shift is maintaining their authenticity. Too often, in an attempt to "keep up," ministries abandon their core message in favor of chasing trends. Here's how to adapt wisely:

A. Diversify Your Content Strategy

Platforms favor different types of content at different times. Rather than relying on a single format, ministries should develop a content ecosystem that includes:

- **Long-form content for deep engagement** (sermons, interviews)

- **Short-form content for discovery** (Reels, TikTok, YouTube Shorts)

- **Live interactions for real-time connection** (Facebook Live, Instagram Q&A)

- **Blog & newsletter integration** for platform independence

Example: Instead of just posting a full sermon, a church could create:

- A short clip highlighting a key quote for Instagram Reels

- A deep-dive blog post for SEO and email newsletters

- A live Q&A session after the service to answer audience questions

- A repurposed segment for YouTube Shorts

This multi-platform approach ensures that if one algorithm shifts, your message still reaches audiences through other channels.

B. Prioritize Relationship Over Reach

Algorithms reward engagement, not just content volume. Faith-based media leaders should focus on **fostering community, not just broadcasting messages**:

- **Ask questions that invite responses** (e.g., "What Bible verse is helping you this week?")

- **Encourage user-generated content** (testimonies, challenges)

- **Reply to comments within the first 30 minutes** to boost ranking

- **Leverage groups and communities** (Facebook Groups, WhatsApp chats)

Example: A ministry that saw engagement drop after a Facebook algorithm change shifted its focus to **group-based discussions**, where the algorithm prioritizes community-driven conversations. The result? Increased reach without relying solely on newsfeed rankings.

3. Future-Proofing Your Faith-Based Media Strategy

With digital landscapes shifting faster than ever, ministries must think long-term. Instead of reacting to every algorithm change, build a strategy that **anticipates trends** and remains adaptable.

A. Invest in Owned Platforms

Social media is a borrowed space—you don't control it. Every ministry should build **direct access channels** such as:

- Email newsletters

- Mobile apps

- Private community platforms (e.g., Mighty Networks, Discord)

- Podcasting (not controlled by one algorithm)

A church that lost 80% of its engagement after an Instagram update **shifted focus to an email-driven discipleship series**— and saw engagement return to pre-algorithm change levels.

B. Stay Agile & Experiment

- Test new platform features **early** (e.g., AI chatbots for engagement, interactive video tools)

- Measure impact with **analytics** (track what works, pivot when needed)

- Learn from secular trends and adapt them for **faith-driven storytelling**

Confidence in the Midst of Change

Faith-based media leaders can't afford to be passive observers in the digital world. By **understanding algorithm changes, adapting content strategies, and future-proofing outreach**, ministries can stay ahead—without compromising their message.

Reflection Questions:

1. How have recent platform changes affected your outreach? Where have you seen the biggest shifts?

2. Are you relying too much on one platform? What steps can you take to diversity your strategy?

3. What new content formats or engagement tactics can you test this month?

Key Takeaway: Faith-driven digital outreach is about **stewardship, not survival**. By combining **innovation with**

authenticity, ministries can turn shifting algorithms into opportunities for greater impact.

Staying Authentic While Scaling Outreach

Introduction

As ministries and faith-based organizations expand their media outreach, maintaining authenticity becomes a critical challenge. Growth brings new opportunities but also increased scrutiny, shifting audience expectations, and the temptation to prioritize reach over genuine connection. In today's digital landscape, authenticity is currency. Audiences—especially younger demographics—demand transparency, consistency, and meaningful engagement. Scaling outreach successfully requires more than just increasing content production and distribution; it necessitates preserving the mission, values, and heart of the ministry.

This chapter explores how ministries and faith-based media leaders can grow their platforms while staying true to their identity. We'll examine the core principles of authenticity, the risks of dilution during expansion, and practical strategies to ensure that growth enhances rather than undermines your message.

The Core of Authenticity in Faith-Based Outreach: What Does Authenticity Mean in Digital Outreach?

Authenticity in media ministry means that the message you share aligns with your mission, values, and how you interact with your audience. It's not just about content consistency but also about maintaining sincerity in messaging, storytelling, and engagement.

Authenticity builds trust and credibility, which are essential for long-term audience retention and impact.

Key components of authenticity include:

- **Consistency** – Does your content reflect your mission across all platforms?

- **Transparency** – Are you honest about your ministry's goals, successes, and struggles?

- **Engagement** – Do you listen to your audience and foster genuine interactions?

- **Integrity** – Are your values evident in both your digital presence and offline ministry?

As ministries scale, these elements can become challenging to maintain. The pressure to increase reach and revenue can sometimes lead to a loss of personal connection or a shift in messaging that prioritizes popularity over purpose.

The Risks of Scaling Too Fast or Losing Authenticity

When Growth Comes at a Cost

Scaling outreach isn't inherently bad—ministries should seek to expand their influence to spread the gospel effectively. However, rapid expansion without a strategic foundation can lead to:

- **Diluted Messaging** – Trying to appeal to a wider audience may lead to content that lacks the depth and mission-driven focus of earlier efforts.

- **Overproduction and Burnout** – Producing content at an unsustainable rate can strain teams, leading to decreased quality and inconsistency.

- **Lack of Engagement** – As the audience grows, personal interaction can suffer. Automated responses and generic messaging replace the relational aspect that originally attracted followers.

- **Brand Confusion** – Expanding across multiple platforms without a unified strategy can result in mixed messaging, making it difficult for audiences to understand your ministry's identity.

By identifying these risks early, faith-based leaders can scale strategically without sacrificing the core of their ministry.

Strategies for Scaling Without Losing Your Identity

1. Root Your Growth in Your Mission

Before expanding into new media channels, revisiting your core mission is essential. Growth should amplify, not redefine, your calling. Ask:

- Does this platform or strategy align with our ministry's core values?

- Will this method enhance engagement or just increase visibility?

- Are we equipped to maintain quality and consistency as we grow?

Every new venture should be measured against your mission. If a media opportunity requires a compromise on your core values, it's not the right fit.

2. Prioritize Depth Over Breadth

Scaling effectively isn't about being on every platform—it's about being where you can be most impactful. Instead of stretching your team thin across multiple channels, focus on:

- Deepening relationships on existing platforms before expanding.

- Strengthening engagement strategies to build a loyal community.

- Repurposing high-value content rather than churning out endless new material.

By maintaining depth, you ensure that growth enhances audience trust instead of replacing meaningful interactions with surface-level content.

3. Leverage Technology Without Losing the Human Touch

Automation and AI tools can help ministries scale, but they should not replace authentic interaction. Strategies for maintaining personal connection while leveraging technology include:

- **Personalized Content** – Use AI-driven insights to tailor messages to different audience segments.

163

- **Live Engagement** – Maintain real-time connection through live Q&As, prayer sessions, or community discussions.

- **Hybrid Models** – Balance automation (for efficiency) with human-led engagement (for authenticity).

Technology should amplify your reach, not depersonalize your ministry.

4. Develop a Scalable Content Strategy That Reflects Your Values

Maintaining authenticity requires a content framework that grows with your audience while staying true to your mission. A scalable content strategy should include:

- **Editorial Consistency** – Develop content guidelines that ensure uniform messaging across all platforms.

- **Purpose-Driven Content Creation** – Each piece of content should serve a specific mission goal—whether to educate, inspire, or mobilize.

- **Cross-Platform Repurposing** – Convert long-form content into shorter clips, blogs, and social posts to maximize impact without diluting your message.

By establishing a structured but flexible strategy, you can ensure your content remains mission-aligned as your audience expands.

5. Stay Accountable with Regular Mission Alignment Check-ins

As ministries scale, it's crucial to conduct periodic mission check-ins. This involves:

- **Team Evaluations** – Assess whether new strategies are enhancing or detracting from your ministry's core values.

- **Audience Feedback** – Gather insights from your community to understand whether they feel connected to your mission.

- **Data & Impact Analysis** – Use analytics not just for reach, but for measuring engagement, transformation, and impact.

Regular alignment checks ensure that growth doesn't lead to mission drift.

Growing with Integrity and Purpose

Scaling outreach is necessary in today's media landscape, but it must be done with intentionality. Ministries and faith-based organizations must guard against the pitfalls of rapid expansion by staying deeply rooted in their mission, prioritizing authentic engagement, and using technology wisely.

By keeping authenticity at the forefront, faith leaders can ensure that as their influence grows, their message remains clear, impactful, and aligned with the gospel. The key to staying authentic while scaling isn't about resisting growth; it's about ensuring that growth strengthens rather than dilutes your calling.

As you expand your reach, remember: true impact isn't measured just in numbers, but in transformed lives. Stay rooted in purpose, engage with sincerity, and let your growth be an extension of God's mission, not a departure from it.

10 The Future of Faith-Based Media

The Next Wave: AI, VR, and the Metaverse in Ministry

The world of media and communication is evolving at an unprecedented pace, and ministries must keep up if they hope to remain relevant. Just as radio and television once revolutionized faith-based outreach, today's advancements in **artificial intelligence (AI), virtual reality (VR), and the Metaverse** are presenting new opportunities—and challenges—for the church.

The pressing question for faith leaders is no longer **whether** to engage with these technologies, but **how** to do so in a way that aligns with their mission and values. How can ministries embrace these tools to **enhance engagement, foster community, and spread the Gospel** without losing the essence of authentic faith-driven outreach?

This chapter will explore the potential of AI, VR, and the Metaverse for ministry, highlighting **real-world applications, ethical considerations, and best practices** for integrating emerging technologies into faith-based media.

1. The Role of AI in Ministry

AI for Content Creation and Personalization

- AI-driven tools can assist in **sermon transcriptions, video captioning, and automated social media posts**.

- AI chatbots can provide **scripture-based responses** to common faith questions.

- Personalized devotionals or sermon recommendations based on **AI-powered behavioral analysis**.

AI for Audience Engagement and Insights

- **Predictive analytics** can identify engagement trends and suggest optimal posting schedules.

- AI-driven **fundraising recommendations** can help ministries optimize donor outreach.

- Automated **prayer support chatbots** can connect users to scriptures and faith-based guidance 24/7.

Ethical Considerations of AI in Ministry

- AI **cannot replace pastoral care**; human connection remains irreplaceable.

- The importance of **ensuring theological accuracy** in AI-generated responses.

- Avoiding over-reliance on automation at the cost of **authentic spiritual engagement**.

2. Virtual Reality (VR) and the Future of Worship

VR Church Services and Immersive Worship

- VR allows for **full church services in a digital environment**, reaching those who cannot attend in person.

- **Live worship experiences** where attendees feel present, even if physically distant.

- Creating **virtual prayer rooms and confession spaces** for more intimate digital ministry.

VR for Bible Study and Discipleship

- Interactive, **immersive Bible stories** where users can experience historical events firsthand.

- **Small groups in VR** can foster deeper conversations in a setting free from geographical constraints.

- **Training programs for pastors and ministry leaders** in a VR classroom setting.

Challenges of VR in Ministry

- **Is digital presence a substitute for physical church community?**

- The risk of **disconnection from real-life relationships.**

- Theological concerns around **sacraments, communion, and virtual baptism.**

3. The Metaverse: A New Mission Field

Understanding the Metaverse as a Cultural Shift

- The Metaverse is **more than just a trend**; it's a shift toward fully digital environments where people interact, work, and worship.

- **Young generations** are spending more time in digital spaces than ever before.

- Ministries can no longer afford to ignore **where people are gathering online**.

How Ministries Can Use the Metaverse for Outreach

- **Virtual churches** with custom-designed spaces for worship, fellowship, and teaching.

- **Faith-based NFT fundraising** to support global missions.

- Digital discipleship programs that guide new believers through **immersive, interactive faith experiences**.

Theological and Ethical Concerns

- Is **virtual worship an acceptable replacement** for physical church gatherings?

- How can ministries **safeguard theological integrity** in digital spaces?

- Addressing concerns around **digital escapism vs. real-world discipleship**.

4. Balancing Innovation with Integrity

Practical Guidelines for Faith Leaders

1. **Adopt wisely:** Ensure that technology **enhances, rather than replaces,** personal faith connections.

2. **Prioritize community:** Use AI, VR, and the Metaverse to **bring people together**, not isolate them.

3. **Stay theologically grounded:** Regularly evaluate whether technological advancements **align with biblical principles**.

4. **Train ministry teams:** Equip leaders with the skills to **responsibly integrate digital tools** into outreach strategies.

Case Studies of Churches and Ministries Pioneering AI, VR, and the Metaverse

- **Life.Church:** Early adopters of **AI-driven engagement** and VR worship services.

- **VR Church:** A fully immersive church that exists **entirely in the Metaverse**, offering weekly services and discipleship programs.

- **YouVersion Bible App:** Uses AI to **personalize devotionals** and scripture recommendations.

Key Takeaways

- AI can enhance **content creation, engagement, and analytics**, but must be used ethically.

- VR enables **immersive worship and learning experiences**, but presents theological challenges.
- The Metaverse is **a new mission field**, requiring ministries to be intentional in outreach.
- Ministries must **balance technological adoption with biblical principles** to maintain authenticity.

Embracing the Future with Purpose

The digital age presents faith-based organizations with **unparalleled opportunities** to reach people in new and engaging ways. However, these advancements come with **ethical, theological, and practical considerations**. By **thoughtfully integrating AI, VR, and Metaverse strategies**, ministries can **expand their reach** while remaining **true to their mission**.

The next chapter, *Building a Media Strategy That Stands the Test of Time*, will explore how ministries can **strategically implement these emerging technologies** in a way that ensures long-term sustainability and faithfulness to the Gospel.

Building a Media Strategy That Stands the Test of Time

The Challenge of Longevity in Faith-Based Media

The digital media landscape is constantly evolving. Ministries and faith-based organizations must balance adaptability with consistency, ensuring that their message remains timeless while their delivery methods stay relevant.

In the previous chapter, we explored AI, VR, and the Metaverse and how emerging technologies are shaping the future of ministry. Now, we shift focus to how faith-based media organizations can build sustainable, long-term strategies that stand strong despite technological disruptions, platform changes, and shifting audience behaviors.

A well-built media strategy is not tied to fleeting trends—it is rooted in a clear mission, an adaptable structure, and a deep understanding of audience needs. This chapter outlines how ministries can construct a resilient and impactful media presence that will thrive for decades to come.

The Core Principles of a Lasting Media Strategy

1. A Clear and Unshakable Mission

Technology will change. Platforms will rise and fall. Your mission must remain firm. Before refining any outreach plan, ask:

- What is our core message?
- How does every media platform serve this mission?
- Are we prioritizing short-term success over long-term impact?

A strong media strategy is mission-driven, not trend-driven. Ministries must avoid chasing short-lived platform trends at the expense of deep, meaningful engagement.

2. Platform-Agnostic Content

Many organizations fail because they build their strategy around a platform rather than a timeless message. A platform-agnostic approach ensures that the message remains effective even as platforms evolve.

- Repurpose content across multiple platforms.

- Avoid over-reliance on any single media channel.

- Ensure flexibility in adapting to new media environments.

Example: Ministries that once thrived on broadcast television are now integrating social media and streaming. The most successful ones preserve their core message while adjusting their delivery methods.

Key Insight: Build a content-first strategy that transcends individual platforms.

3. The Evergreen and Adaptive Content Model

Sustainable media strategies balance two types of content:

Evergreen Content

- Timeless teachings that remain relevant over the years.

- Can be repurposed across platforms.

- Builds a long-term content library for future use.

Adaptive Content

- Responds to cultural shifts, technology changes, and audience engagement trends.

- Incorporates current events and platform updates.

- Ensures ongoing engagement without abandoning foundational messages.

Example: A five-year-old sermon series can be repurposed into:

- A podcast series

- Short-form YouTube videos

- Email-based devotionals

- A faith-based online course

Quick Win: Audit your content library and identify materials that can be repurposed without full reinvention.

Preparing for Future Media Disruptions

The digital landscape is unpredictable. Faith-based media leaders must be proactive, ensuring that their organizations can pivot when necessary.

1. Own Your Audience Relationship

Many ministries have suffered dramatic audience losses due to algorithm changes on social media platforms. The best way to future-proof your strategy is to own your audience data through:

- Email Lists – Direct access to supporters.

- Membership Platforms – Private online communities.

- SMS/Text Engagement – Personalized, direct outreach.

Action Step: Conduct a "What If" analysis how would your media presence survive if a major platform disappeared tomorrow?

2. The "Kingdom ROI" Mindset

Traditional media measures success with numbers: views, shares, likes, and subscriptions. While these metrics matter, a faith-based media strategy must prioritize:

- Are we reaching the right people, not just the most people?

- Are we fostering true engagement, not just passive consumption?

- Are we equipping and discipling viewers, not just entertaining them?

Key Insight: Ministries should prioritize depth of engagement over superficial reach.

Sustaining the Next Generation of Faith-Based Media Leaders

The longest-lasting ministries are those that invest in the next generation. Media strategies should include leadership training to ensure that future leaders can carry the vision forward.

Developing Future Media Leaders

Practical Ways to Train New Faith-Based Media Professionals:

- Internships and Fellowship Programs – Develop the next generation of digital ministry leaders.

- Ongoing Digital Training – Equip teams with AI, VR, and Web3 knowledge to prepare for future trends.

- Mentorship and Succession Planning – Identify future leaders and provide hands-on training.

Action Step: If your leadership team transitioned today, would they have the skills and vision to continue your mission?

The Blueprint for a Long-Lasting Media Strategy

A faith-based media strategy that stands the test of time must:

- Be mission-driven—unwavering in core values.

- Use a platform-agnostic approach—adaptable across media shifts.

- Balance evergreen and adaptive content—creating both timeless and relevant materials.

- Be prepared for disruptions—ensuring long-term sustainability.

- Prioritize Kingdom impact over fleeting success.

- Invest in future faith-based media leaders—training the next generation.

The future of faith-based media belongs to those who remain deeply rooted in their mission while boldly innovating for the next era.

Equipping the Next Generation of Faith-Based Media Leaders

The Urgency of Leadership Development

Faith-based media is at a critical juncture. While many visionary leaders have pioneered the integration of social media, streaming, broadcast, and cable, a pressing question looms: Who will carry the torch forward? Ministries that fail to equip new leaders risk stagnation or even dissolution. The rapid pace of technological advancement demands adaptable, forward-thinking media leadership that remains grounded in biblical truth.

A lack of leadership transition planning can create a vacuum where faith-based media efforts lose momentum. However, when today's leaders actively mentor and train the next generation, the impact of faith-driven media not only endures but expands. Investing in leadership development ensures that future media leaders continue spreading the gospel effectively through evolving digital platforms.

Mentorship & Discipleship in Media Leadership

Biblical leadership is not transactional—it is relational. Jesus modeled mentorship through discipleship, investing in a few so they could reach the many. This principle applies to faith-based media as well. Senior media leaders must see themselves not just as content creators but as mentors responsible for shaping the next wave of faith-driven storytellers and communicators.

Practical Ways to Mentor New Leaders:

- **Create Internship & Apprenticeship Programs**: Hands-on experience is invaluable. Provide structured opportunities for emerging media leaders to learn the technical, strategic, and spiritual aspects of faith-based media.

- **Develop Leadership Networks**: Establish mentorship groups where seasoned professionals can guide and support newcomers.

- **Offer Training & Workshops**: From digital storytelling to media ethics, ongoing education ensures that new leaders are well-equipped to navigate challenges.

- **Encourage Cross-Generational Collaboration**: Pair experienced media professionals with younger talent to foster knowledge exchange and innovation.

Case Study: A well-established Christian media organization saw a 40% increase in digital engagement after launching a mentorship initiative that paired veteran content creators with new digital strategists. The fresh insights from younger team members, combined with the wisdom of experienced leaders, created a dynamic approach to media outreach.

Training for the Digital Age

Equipping future leaders goes beyond mentorship—it requires intentional training in both technology and storytelling. While theological education is important, media leaders must also master the tools and techniques necessary to engage today's digital-first audience.

Key Training Areas:

1. **Technical Proficiency**
   - Video production and editing for streaming platforms

- o Social media strategy and audience engagement

- o Data analytics to optimize outreach effectiveness

2. **Content Creation & Storytelling**

   - o Crafting compelling narratives that resonate across generations

   - o Utilizing short-form and long-form content effectively

   - o Understanding cross-platform content repurposing

3. **Strategic & Ethical Leadership**

   - o Balancing innovation with biblical integrity

   - o Navigating censorship, platform shifts, and content restrictions

   - o Implementing sustainable business models for faith-based media

Faith-based organizations should consider partnerships with universities, digital marketing firms, and tech innovators to create certification programs that equip new leaders with both spiritual and technical acumen.

The Mindset of a Media Leader

Beyond technical skills, faith-based media leaders must cultivate a mindset rooted in spiritual resilience, ethical responsibility, and cultural awareness. The next generation must understand that they are not merely content distributors; they are stewards of a message that transforms lives.

Characteristics of an Effective Faith-Based Media Leader:

- **Spirit-Led Vision**: Anchoring media strategy in prayer and biblical truth.

- **Cultural Awareness**: Engaging audiences in ways that are relevant and relatable.

- **Ethical Integrity**: Upholding biblical values in media practices.

- **Adaptability & Innovation**: Embracing new technology while preserving the core message of the gospel.

Encouraging innovation while maintaining theological consistency requires a delicate balance. Leaders must be flexible enough to leverage AI, Web3, and emerging media trends without compromising the foundational principles of faith-driven communication.

Passing the Torch: Creating a Culture of Continuous Learning

Leadership is not a destination; it is a journey. The next generation of faith-based media leaders must be cultivated through continuous learning, not just a one-time training event. Ministries should instill a culture of ongoing development by:

- **Hosting Leadership Summits**: Regular gatherings where media leaders share insights and strategies.

- **Implementing Rotational Leadership Models**: Allowing young leaders to take on key roles under the guidance of mentors.

- **Encouraging Lifelong Learning**: Providing access to industry conferences, certifications, and theological training.

Organizations that successfully equip emerging leaders will see long-term sustainability. The effectiveness of faith-based media depends not only on today's decisions but on tomorrow's leaders being prepared to continue the mission.

Equipping the next generation of faith-based media leaders is not optional—it is essential. Ministries and organizations must take proactive steps to train, mentor, and empower emerging leaders.

Practical Steps for Today's Leaders:

1. Identify 2-3 emerging media leaders in your organization or network.

2. Begin a structured mentorship plan with them, focusing on both technical skills and spiritual leadership.

3. Integrate leadership development into your media strategy, ensuring long-term sustainability.

4. Establish training programs that blend theological depth with media expertise.

5. Encourage a culture of continuous learning through peer mentorship and collaborative projects.

The future of faith-based media depends on the leaders we equip today. By investing in the next generation, we ensure that the message of hope, faith, and salvation continues to reach hearts across every media platform. The call is clear: Train up leaders who are spiritually strong, technically skilled, and passionately committed to sharing the gospel through media. In doing so, we are not just preserving a legacy—we are expanding the kingdom impact for generations to come.

Lee Allen Miller

11 Implementation Roadmap

Steps to Building Your Media Empire: Defining Your Vision and Mission

Before diving into building a media empire, ministries and faith-based media leaders must first establish a **clear vision and mission**. Without a defined purpose, media strategies can become scattered and ineffective. Ask yourself:

- What is the core message of our ministry?

- Who is our target audience?

- What platforms align best with our goals?

- How do we want to impact our community?

Once this vision is established, craft a concise mission statement that will guide every media decision moving forward.

Assessing Your Current Media Presence

Understanding where you currently stand is critical before expanding your media reach. Conduct a **media audit** by evaluating:

- Your website's effectiveness and user experience

- Social media engagement levels

- Streaming presence and viewership analytics

- Broadcast and cable partnerships

- Current content strategy (strengths and gaps)

- SEO rankings and digital discoverability

With this data, identify strengths, weaknesses, opportunities, and threats (SWOT analysis) to shape your next steps.

Creating a Multi-Platform Content Strategy

A successful media empire requires content that is **repurposed and adapted** for various platforms while maintaining a consistent message. Consider these key elements:

- **Content Pillars** – Identify 3-5 key themes your content will revolve around.

- **Platform Optimization** – Adjust formats for each channel (e.g., short clips for social, long-form for YouTube, high-quality for broadcast).

- **Editorial Calendar** – Develop a posting schedule that ensures consistency across all platforms.

- **Live vs. Pre-Recorded Balance** – Utilize live streaming for real-time engagement and pre-recorded content for polished messaging.

Building a Strong Digital Infrastructure

Your media empire requires a **robust digital foundation** This includes:

- A **mobile-friendly, high-performing website** that serves as the central hub

- Secure and scalable **streaming capabilities**

- **CRM and email marketing tools** to nurture engagement

- **SEO and digital ads strategy** for audience growth

- **AI and automation tools** to streamline operations

Developing a Sustainable Production Workflow

Consistency is key, but it must be sustainable. Develop a workflow that maximizes efficiency while maintaining quality. Steps include:

1. **Content Ideation & Planning** – Brainstorm content ideas aligned with your mission.

2. **Scripting & Pre-Production** – Outline messaging and gather assets.

3. **Production & Recording** – Invest in quality visuals and audio.

4. **Post-Production & Editing** – Ensure high production value.

5. **Distribution & Scheduling** – Use scheduling tools to maintain consistency.

6. **Performance Tracking & Optimization** – Analyze data and refine strategies.

Engaging the Audience Effectively

Media is not a one-way street. Faith-based media leaders must **foster two-way engagement** with their audience. This includes:

- Responding to comments and messages

- Hosting live Q&A sessions

- Encouraging user-generated content (testimonies, testimonials)

- Creating online communities or discussion groups

- Utilizing interactive elements like polls, quizzes, and challenges

Monetization and Sustainability Strategies

While mission-driven, media empires must remain financially viable. Consider sustainable funding options such as:

- **Digital Giving & Donations** – Encourage online tithing and crowdfunding.

- **Subscription Models** – Offer exclusive content for members.

- **Sponsorship & Advertising** – Partner with brands that align with your values.

- **Merchandising** – Create faith-based products that engage audiences.

- **Speaking Engagements & Courses** – Share expertise through paid events.

Scaling the Media Presence with a Leadership Model

Growth requires a **structured leadership approach**. Consider:

- **Delegating Responsibilities** – Assigning roles for content creation, engagement, analytics, and sponsorships.

- **Training & Development** – Equipping team members with media skills.

- **Building Strategic Partnerships** – Collaborating with other ministries, networks, and tech providers.

- **Expanding Distribution Channels** – Exploring syndication and cross-platform growth opportunities.

Moving Forward with Confidence

Building a faith-based media empire requires a **strategic, purpose-driven approach**. By defining your mission, assessing your current media presence, optimizing content strategy, investing in digital infrastructure, and engaging audiences effectively, you set the stage for long-term success.

This structured approach ensures that ministries are not just broadcasting their message, but truly **connecting, engaging, and transforming** lives through an integrated media empire.

Checklist for Integrating Social, Streaming, Broadcast, and Cable

Why Integration Matters

Faith-based organizations often struggle with siloed media strategies. Social media, streaming, broadcast, and cable are powerful tools, but without a unified approach, their impact is diluted. This checklist ensures that ministries and Christian media leaders move from isolated efforts to a seamless, cohesive media strategy.

Step 1: Define Your Core Media Message

- ☐ Identify the overarching mission of your media strategy.

- ☐ Develop a clear and consistent message that resonates across all platforms.

- ☐ Ensure messaging aligns with your ministry's values and long-term goals.

- ☐ Create a style guide for visuals, language, and tone to maintain uniformity.

Step 2: Align Your Audience with the Right Platforms

- ☐ Determine key audience demographics (age, interests, viewing habits).

- ☐ Map audience preferences to platforms (e.g., younger viewers on YouTube & Instagram, older audiences on broadcast & cable).

- ☐ Use engagement data to refine platform selection and priorities.

Step 3: Optimize Content for Each Medium

- ☐ Social Media: Short-form, interactive content (clips, reels, polls).

- ☐ Streaming: High-quality sermons, podcasts, and live events.

- ☐ Broadcast: Longer-form, traditional programming adapted for digital use.

- ☐ Cable: Syndication strategies for reaching regional and national audiences.

Step 4: Develop a Content Distribution Plan

- ☐ Identify core content pieces that can be repurposed across multiple platforms.

- ☐ Use a content calendar to coordinate publishing across social, streaming, and broadcast.

- ☐ Leverage AI-driven scheduling tools for consistency.

- ☐ Implement a cross-promotion strategy to drive viewers from one platform to another.

Step 5: Invest in a Sustainable Workflow

- ☐ Build an internal team or work with partners to manage content production.

- ☐ Create efficient recording, editing, and repurposing workflows.

- ☐ Standardize file formats and resolutions to ensure compatibility across platforms.

- ☐ Automate routine tasks such as social media scheduling and email marketing.

Step 6: Leverage Technology for Engagement & Growth

- ☐ Implement AI tools for social media engagement and content personalization.

- ☐ Explore Web3 opportunities for faith-based fundraising.

- ☐ Use data analytics to refine outreach strategies.

- ☐ Optimize video titles, thumbnails, and metadata for searchability.

Step 7: Monetization and Funding Strategies

- ☐ Introduce digital giving options (text-to-give, QR codes, online donations).

- ☐ Experiment with subscription models for premium content.

- ☐ Use ad revenue and sponsorships strategically on social and streaming platforms.

- ☐ Explore syndication deals to maximize revenue from broadcast and cable.

Step 8: Build Community and Two-Way Engagement

- ☐ Encourage audience participation through comments, live chats, and social groups.

- ☐ Develop a follow-up strategy for first-time viewers to deepen engagement.

- ☐ Organize digital discipleship programs and interactive livestreams.

- ☐ Use email and text-based communication to maintain connection with followers.

Step 9: Measure Success and Adapt

- ☐ Track KPIs such as viewership, engagement, and donation conversion rates.

- ☐ Regularly review audience insights to refine content strategies.

- ☐ Test and iterate: What's working? What needs adjustment?

- ☐ Conduct annual reviews to align strategy with evolving media trends.

Moving from Strategy to Action

This checklist transforms fragmented media efforts into a powerful, cohesive strategy. Ministries that embrace integration will see greater engagement, deeper audience connection, and increased impact.

Case Studies of Successful Faith-Based Media Strategies: Introduction: Learning from Proven Models

Implementing a successful media strategy that unifies social, streaming, broadcast, and cable requires more than just theory—it demands real-world application. In this chapter, we explore case studies of faith-based organizations that have effectively integrated these platforms, providing valuable insights and actionable takeaways.

Case Study 1: Elevation Church – A Multi-Platform Powerhouse

Overview:

Elevation Church, led by Pastor Steven Furtick, has successfully bridged digital and traditional media. By utilizing a combination of live streaming, social media engagement, cable syndication, and YouTube optimization, they have built a powerful outreach model.

Key Strategies:

- **YouTube as a Content Hub:** Elevation Church repurposes its sermons, worship segments, and leadership talks into shorter, engaging clips that generate millions of views.

- **Live Streaming Excellence:** Their high-production-value live streams offer seamless experiences across their website, social platforms, and mobile apps.

- **Cable & Broadcast Partnerships:** Elevation's sermons air on major Christian television networks, ensuring traditional media reach complements their digital strategy.

- **Engagement-Driven Social Media:** They prioritize high-quality graphics, sermon highlights, and interactive Q&A sessions to create ongoing conversations with their audience.

Lessons Learned:

- High-quality, multi-purpose content increases reach and engagement.

- Syndication across platforms ensures longevity and accessibility.

- Community interaction fosters loyalty and deeper audience connections.

Case Study 2: Life.Church – The Digital-First Ministry

Overview:

Life.Church, known for launching the Bible App (YouVersion), has successfully adopted a digital-first strategy that integrates social media, streaming, and broadcast television.

Key Strategies:

- **On-Demand Streaming:** Sermons are available on-demand, allowing users to engage at their convenience.

- **Interactive Live Experiences:** Live streaming services include real-time chat, prayer requests, and virtual community groups.

- **Mobile-First Approach:** Life.Church prioritizes mobile accessibility, ensuring engagement through apps and mobile-friendly content.

- **Broadcast Integration:** Partnering with Christian television networks extends their message to a broader audience.

Lessons Learned:

- A mobile-first mindset expands global reach.

- Interactive live streams deepen community engagement.

- App-based engagement fosters sustained audience retention.

Case Study 3: TBN's Digital Reinvention

Overview:

Trinity Broadcasting Network (TBN), once purely a traditional broadcast powerhouse, has successfully adapted to the digital age by integrating streaming services and social media outreach.

Key Strategies:

- **TBN+ Streaming Platform:** Offers on-demand access to sermons, documentaries, and original faith-based shows.

- **Social Media Resurgence:** Focus on bite-sized clips and influencer collaborations to engage younger audiences.

- **OTT Expansion:** Partnering with platforms like Roku and Apple TV has allowed them to reach cord-cutters.

Lessons Learned:

- Transitioning from traditional to digital requires a strong investment in content repurposing.

- Partnering with new media platforms increases accessibility.

- Faith-based streaming services can compete with mainstream digital entertainment.

Case Study 4: Transformation Church – Leveraging Viral Moments

Overview:

Pastor Michael Todd's Transformation Church exemplifies how faith-based content can go viral, attracting a global audience through intentional storytelling and digital excellence.

Key Strategies:

- **Social Media-Driven Growth:** Viral sermon clips on Instagram, TikTok, and YouTube Shorts attract millions of views.

- **Authenticity & Relevance:** Michael Todd connects with audiences using culturally relevant messages and dynamic delivery.

- **High-Quality Production:** A cinematic approach to live streams and video content sets them apart.

Lessons Learned:

- Viral content needs authenticity and high engagement value.

- Multi-platform consistency maximizes outreach.

- Investing in professional-quality video production pays off.

Case Study 5: The Chosen – Crowdfunded Media Revolution

Overview:

The Chosen, the first-ever multi-season series about the life of Jesus, disrupted traditional Christian media by utilizing a crowdfunding model and a free-to-watch approach.

Key Strategies:

- **Crowdfunding Model:** Over $40 million raised through grassroots funding.

- **Streaming & Social Media Integration:** Distributed via The Chosen app, YouTube, and select broadcast networks.

- **Community-Driven Marketing:** Fans actively share and promote the series, creating organic growth.

Lessons Learned:

- Crowdfunding can work for large-scale faith-based productions.

- Free access increases global reach and impact.

- Community involvement fosters passionate brand evangelists.

Key Takeaways: Lessons from Case Studies

1. **Diversify Content Distribution:** Successful faith-based media organizations leverage multiple platforms, from YouTube to cable syndication.

2. **Engagement Over Broadcasting:** Interaction (social media Q&A, live chat) strengthens audience relationships.

3. **Quality Production Matters:** High production value enhances credibility and retention.

4. **Be Open to New Models:** Crowdfunding, digital-first approaches, and app-based strategies can break traditional limitations.

5. **Leverage Technology:** AI, Web3, and OTT platforms are reshaping faith media's future (setting up for the next chapter).

Looking Ahead: Preparing for the Next Wave

As we transition into the future of faith-based media, these case studies illustrate the necessity of adaptation, innovation, and strategic media integration

The success of these organizations underscores a powerful truth—faith-based media can thrive in a digital-first world when strategy, authenticity, and engagement converge. Whether you're a small ministry or a large broadcasting network, these case studies serve as a roadmap to navigate and maximize your media presence for impactful outreach.

12 That's a Wrap: Empowering the Future of Faith Media Outreach

In the rapidly evolving landscape of media, the need for ministries and faith-based organizations to adapt is more pressing than ever before. From traditional broadcast and cable to social media, streaming, and emerging technologies like AI and Web3, the digital transformation of media is not optional—it's essential for relevance, sustainability, and impact.

Throughout this journey, we have explored the power of integrating social media, streaming platforms, broadcast, and cable into a unified outreach strategy. The message has been clear: to reach the growing global audience of today, faith-based organizations must engage with the full spectrum of media, leveraging the strengths of each platform to tell their stories, share the Gospel, and build communities of believers who are engaged, inspired, and motivated to take action.

The process of digital transformation may seem daunting. The complexity of integrating these diverse platforms often causes hesitation, with many ministries feeling overwhelmed or uncertain about where to begin. But the reality is this: those who embrace this transformation will not only survive but thrive. The opportunity to make a lasting impact through a cohesive media strategy is greater than ever before. And with the right tools, strategies, and mindset, faith-based organizations can unlock the full potential of their outreach.

Actionable Takeaways

1. **Commit to Digital Integration**: Stop over-relying on any single media platform, whether it's social media, broadcast, or cable. Instead, leverage the unique strengths of each medium and create a seamless, unified outreach strategy.

2. **Tell Stories that Resonate**: As Phil Cooke emphasized, compelling storytelling is key to engaging audiences across all platforms. Craft stories that speak to today's cultural context and that deeply resonate with modern-day challenges and aspirations.

3. **Repurpose and Optimize Content**: Whether it's a live-streamed sermon, a podcast, or a YouTube video, repurpose content to reach your audience on various platforms. Consistency in messaging is crucial to maintaining engagementCore

4. **Embrace Emerging Technologies**: Explore the potential of AI, Web3, and blockchain in ministry. These tools offer new ways to engage, fundraise, and create innovative media experiences

5. **Foster Community Engagement**: Move from simply broadcasting your message to fostering two-way conversations. Engage your audience, listen to their

needs, and create spaces for meaningful interaction
Structured Outline

Reflecting on the Road Ahead

As you reflect on the principles and strategies presented, ask yourself: **What steps can I take today to begin uniting my ministry's media platforms?** This is not a journey for the faint-hearted. There will be challenges, but there will also be unprecedented opportunities for growth, transformation, and impact. Your ministry can be part of a faith-based media revolution that not only reaches audiences but nurtures communities, fosters authentic engagement, and shares the hope of Christ across the globe.

The journey ahead requires both faith and action. The world of media is vast and often unpredictable, but it is also filled with untapped potential waiting to be harnessed for the Kingdom of God. As you move forward, remember that digital transformation is not about keeping up with the trends—it's about staying true to your mission and using every tool available to extend the reach of your message.

The future of faith-based media is in your hands. With prayer, strategy, and a commitment to innovation, your ministry can become a powerhouse of outreach that connects with people in ways that were once unimaginable.

Lee Allen Miller

Workshop Speakers & Industry Experts

Phil Cooke

- **Expertise**: Media producer, consultant, and author specializing in faith-based media integration.

- **Key Insights**:

  o Advocates for creativity in Christian media to engage contemporary audiences.

  o Stresses the importance of storytelling and authenticity in media outreach.

  o Encourages ministries to adapt to digital-first strategies without losing their message.

- **Website**: PhilCooke.com

Michael Clarke

- **Role**: Executive Director, *Pathway to Victory* (First Baptist Dallas).

- **Background**:

  o Over 30 years in international faith-based media leadership.

  o Author of *Canada: Portraits of Faith*.

  o Former franchise owner (McDonald's & Dairy Queen).

- **Key Contributions**:

  o Led *Pathway to Victory* to become the top-rated program on Trinity Broadcasting Network (TBN).

- Expertise in integrating traditional broadcasting with modern digital platforms.

- **Website**: PTV.org

Nils Smith

- **Role**: Chief Strategist of Social Media & Innovation at *Dunham+Company*.

- **Specialties**:

  - Social media, streaming, and Web3 technologies in faith-based outreach.

  - AI-driven engagement strategies for ministries.

  - Crypto and blockchain applications for fundraising.

- **Key Insights**:

  - Encourages ministries to view social media as their "front door."

  - Champions live streaming for global audience engagement.

  - Advocates for Web3 and AI to enhance faith-based content distribution.

- **Website**: DunhamandCompany.com

About the Author

Lee Allen Miller is an accomplished entrepreneur, leader, and faith-driven business owner who has dedicated his career to building companies that not only thrive but reflect God's love, integrity, and purpose. As the founder of multiple successful businesses, including MSGPR, Lee brings decades of experience to his work, blending a strong work ethic with a heart for service and a commitment to excellence.

Raised with a foundation in faith and resilience, Lee credits much of his character and drive to the influences of his father, Truitt Miller, who modeled hard work and dedication, and his father-in-law, Ken Cochran, whose unwavering belief in him and deep faith have been a constant source of encouragement. These mentors inspired Lee to lead with purpose, valuing relationships over profit and integrity over convenience. In his journey as a business leader, Lee has found that success comes not only from strategy and skill but from a deep trust in God's guidance, even when the path isn't clear.

Through his writing, Lee aims to share the principles that have shaped his life and work, offering practical insights for entrepreneurs who want to build businesses that honor their faith and impact their communities. His passion for empowering others has made him a respected voice among faith-based entrepreneurs and leaders who strive to create lasting legacies.

Outside of his professional life, Lee cherishes time with his family, finds renewal in his faith, and is dedicated to supporting the growth of fellow entrepreneurs. His journey, marked by resilience, purpose, and an enduring commitment to God, continues to inspire those around him. This book is a testament to his belief that when faith and business intersect, remarkable things are possible.

You can reach out to him at https://msgresources.com .

www.ingramcontent.com/pod-product-compliance
Lightning Source LLC
LaVergne TN
LVHW051230050326
832903LV00028B/2326